GRILL IT!

100 Easy Recipes for Foods to Sear,

Sizzle, and Smoke

GRILL IT!

100 Easy Recipes for Foods to Sear,
Sizzle, and Smoke

Edited by Annette Yates

COURAGE
BOOKS

AN IMPRINT OF RUNNING PRESS
PHILADELPHIA • LONDON

A QUINTET BOOK

9 8 7 6 5 4 3 2 1

Digit on the right indicates the number
of this printing

ISBN 0-7624-0466-3

Library of Congress
Cataloging-in-Publication Number
98-72528

This book was designed and produced by
Quintet Publishing Limited
6 Blundell Street
London N7 9BH

Creative Director: Richard Dewing
Designer: Norma Martin
Art Director: Silke Braun
Project Editor: Amanda Dixon
Editor: Deborah Gray
Photographer: Tim Ferguson Hill
Food Stylists: Kathryn Hawkins and Eliza Baird

Typeset in Great Britain by
Central Southern Typesetters, Eastbourne
Manufactured in Singapore by Universal Graphics Pte Ltd
Printed in China by Leefung Asco Printers Trading Ltd

Published by Courage Books, an imprint of
Running Press Book Publishers
125 South Twenty-Second Street
Philadelphia, Pennsylvania 19103-4399

Recipes in this book have appeared in previous Quintet titles by other
authors, and have been edited by Deborah Gray for this edition.
New recipes were compiled by Annette Yates.

CONTENTS

INTRODUCTION

Nothing evokes memories of the great outdoors and long, summer days more than the mouthwatering smell of dinner cooking on burnishing coals. Sometimes a simple hamburger or plain cooked steak is just right for the occasion, while at other times we prefer a more sophisticated cookout meal. Grill It! has all the recipes that you need to turn simple food into elegant cuisine without spending hours on preparation. With crafty use of marinades, spice rubs, and a host of fresh ingredients enhanced by the smoke of the grill, you can create meals in the back yard as impressive as those at any steakhouse.

THE KEY TO A SUCCESSFUL BARBECUE PARTY IS BEING ORGANIZED AND EFFICIENT, WHICH IN TURN GIVES RISE TO A CALM AND CONFIDENT COOK. HAVE READY PLENTY OF FOODS TO OFFER YOUR GUESTS WHILE THE GRILL IS HEATING UP, AND TO TAKE THE EDGE OFF THEIR HUNGER AS THEY SMELL THE FOOD COOKING. DIPS, SALADS, BREADS, AND APPETIZERS SHOULD BE PLACED ON A TABLE AWAY FROM THE GRILL. HAVE A SEPARATE TABLE, IF POSSIBLE, FOR DRINKS AND GLASSES, AND PLENTY OF PLACES HANDY FOR PEOPLE TO REST THEIR PLATES.

IT IS ALSO ESSENTIAL TO HAVE THE GRILL PREHEATED TO THE CORRECT TEMPERATURE BEFORE STARTING TO COOK, OR YOU RISK HAVING FOOD THAT IS CHARRED ON THE OUTSIDE AND UNDERCOOKED IN THE MIDDLE, OR DRIED-OUT FOOD THAT HAS SLOW-COOKED FOR TOO LONG. TRY THE SIMPLE HAND TEST TO GAUGE THE TEMPERATURE. HOLD YOUR HAND ABOUT FIVE INCHES AWAY FROM THE COOKING SURFACE. IF YOU CAN HOLD IT THERE FOR ONE OR TWO SECONDS, YOU HAVE A HOT FIRE; THREE TO FIVE SECONDS MEANS A MEDIUM FIRE; SIX TO EIGHT SECONDS (WITH NO GLOWING COALS) IS COOL. WHEN YOU WANT A COOL FIRE (PERHAPS FOR COOKING FRUIT OR EMBER-COOKED VEGETABLES), IT'S BEST TO LET THE CHARCOAL BURN FOR LONGER AND DIE DOWN A LITTLE.

SO, SET TO IT—GRILL IT!

Chapter 1

PORTABLE GRILL

Light up the Fire
The Right Equipment

Your basic choice is between charcoal and gas. There are those who would not be persuaded to use anything other than charcoal, because for them the building, lighting, and nurturing of the fire are all part of the occasion. Others prefer the immediacy of a gas grill, which is usually ready to use about ten minutes after lighting. No matter which you choose, the food will have that recognizable "cooked-outdoors" flavor.

Barbecue Designs

DISPOSABLE GRILLS These are small and inexpensive, designed to be disposed of after use. They are great for small spaces or for a spontaneous barbecue for two, whether in the yard, on the deck, on the beach, or at a campsite. A thin metal grid sits over a foil tray containing charcoal that has been impregnated with lighter fuel. They are easy to light, ready to use in about 15 minutes, and last for about an hour. The best foods to cook on them are small, thin pieces such as burgers, sausages, vegetables, and kebobs. These are also a good buy for people trying barbecuing for the first time.

PORTABLE GRILLS
There are four basic designs available:
THE HIBACHI (Japanese for fire bowl) has a sturdy, shallow metal tray on short legs or feet, with one or more cooking grids on top. The height of the grids can be adjusted, by slotting them into different notches, and they often have convenient wooden handles.

FOLD-AWAY GRILL

FOLD-AWAY GRILLS are lightweight, easy to store, and easy to assemble.

BUCKET GRILLS are just what they say: a metal bucket with a grid placed on the top.

CONVERTIBLE GRILLS have hot coals sitting below the cooking grid, which can be moved into a vertical position to create a back burner for rotisserie cooking.

FREE-STANDING GRILLS These come in various designs and are made up of a fire bowl on legs with a cooking grid above, which is usually adjustable. The cooking area is larger than that of the portable types. Some have lids, some do not. Kettle, barrel, and pedestal or pillar grills are the most efficient. They are easy to light, quick to reach cooking temperature, and the ventilation can be adjusted to control the rate at which the coals burn. All of them are ideal for the garden.

WAGON OR TROLLEY GRILLS These are generally large and come in designs that vary from the simple to the glamorous, with or without lids, with some or many utensils and shelves. What they all have in common are wheels that allow you to push them, wheelbarrow style, to where you want to cook. These grills are perfect for outdoor parties.

PERMANENT GRILLS A brick-built grill makes barbecuing part of your everyday life. It's ideal where the summer weather is guaranteed to be warm and dry. It also provides an attractive garden feature. The cooking space can be as large and as adjustable as you like, and you can build in shelves, ovens, and storage areas. Simple do-it-yourself kits are available. Cement the bricks to make a permanent barbecue area; stack them for one that can be dismantled at any time.

DISPOSABLE GRILL

BUCKET GRILL

Buying a Grill

COOKING SPACE For regular barbecuers, it's important to have a grill area that is larger than you think you need. Even if you cook only small quantities of food, it allows you to move the food around, to hotter or cooler areas or away from flare-ups. You can move the coals around, too, to create hotter or cooler cooking areas.

ADJUSTABLE GRID HEIGHTS These enable you to adjust the cooking temperature by moving the food closer to or further away from the heat. For the same reason, if you choose the gas variety, it's helpful to be able to adjust the gas flow. The bars on the cooking grids should be sturdy and not so far apart that the food may fall through.

SAFETY Ensure the barbecue is stable; a wobbly model is dangerous. Handles should always be made of wood or a heat-resistant plastic.

LIDS Models with lids are the most versatile, allowing you to grill conventionally or cook the food covered. If you choose a model with a lid, ensure it is deep enough to contain the largest bird or piece of meat that you will want to cook.

CLEANING AND STORAGE Is the barbecue you are thinking of buying easy to clean? You will avoid hours of frustration if it is. You may also need to store the grill somewhere during the winter. Take this into account when choosing.

FREE-STANDING GRILL

TROLLEY GRILL

KETTLE GRILL—A TYPE OF TROLLEY GRILL

Fuel

There are various types of barbecue fuel, each of which has its own advantages and disadvantages—and each of which affects the flavor of the food in a different way. They are wood, charcoal, charcoal briquettes, and gas.

WOOD is still preferred by many people for both the flavor it produces in the food and the aroma of the wood smoke. Well-dried hardwoods are the most usual choice, as many softwoods add unwanted resinous flavors to the food—although if you like retsina (Greek wine flavored with pine-resin), you might like to try cooking with pine chips.

The most usual wood employed is oak, closely followed by hickory, but you can use almost any type. Mesquite, which is often used after it has been turned into charcoal, is not good for a fire: it crackles and spits a lot.

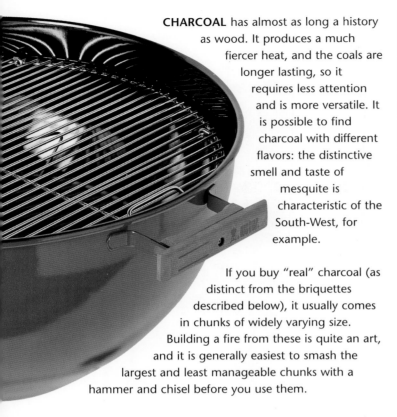

CHARCOAL has almost as long a history as wood. It produces a much fiercer heat, and the coals are longer lasting, so it requires less attention and is more versatile. It is possible to find charcoal with different flavors: the distinctive smell and taste of mesquite is characteristic of the South-West, for example.

If you buy "real" charcoal (as distinct from the briquettes described below), it usually comes in chunks of widely varying size. Building a fire from these is quite an art, and it is generally easiest to smash the largest and least manageable chunks with a hammer and chisel before you use them.

CHARCOAL BRIQUETTES are probably the most popular and convenient of barbecue fuels. One problem with briquettes, however, is that some brands impart a faint chemical taste to the food; this comes from the "mastic" that is used to bind the powdered charcoal. You can't really taste it if you drown the food in sugary commercial barbecue sauce, but if you have spent hours preparing delicately marinated food, it is worth remembering. For this reason, those who care passionately about barbecues rarely use them. If they do, they test several different brands until they find one which cooks like real charcoal. In addition to plain briquettes, you can also get briquettes with a touch of mesquite, and even some made from old Jack Daniels whiskey barrels!

GAS This is usually liquid petroleum gas (LPG) in the form of butane or propane. Butane is the more frequently used, particularly in warm weather. In cooler conditions it is advisable to use propane, which operates well in low temperatures. Natural gas may also be available and comes in handy cylinders. If your home has a mains gas supply, it is possible to have an outside fitting for a barbecue, though this does mean that the barbecue will have to be used close to the house.

In a gas grill, the flame heats up chunks of lava rock or metal plates or bars. These, in turn, heat the food on the cooking grid above.

Tools and Equipment

Although you won't need many complicated tools for the grill, there are a few essentials.

HEAVY-DUTY LONG-HANDLED TONGS AND FORK The tongs make it easier to manipulate the food without

LUMPWOOD CHARCOAL, SPREAD EVENLY

prodding it with a fork and allowing precious juices to escape. A long-handled fork is a useful companion to tongs.

SPATULA A long-handled metal spatula is useful for turning foods such as hamburgers.

BASTING OR MOPPING BRUSHES Essential for basting the food during the cooking process. Make sure the handle is long enough to allow you to work over the fire without burning your forearms.

A THICK APRON AND OVEN OR GARDENING GLOVES

HEAVY-DUTY ALUMINUM FOIL Wrap around chicken wings or other small parts of larger cuts to avoid charring. Also use as a parcel wrap, drip pans, and for keeping cooked food warm.

WATER-SPRAYER Used to suppress flare-ups. A water sprayer is essential if you want to cook large cuts of fatty meat.

METAL AND BAMBOO SKEWERS The best metal skewers are the flat type which prevent the food from slipping as you turn it on the grill. Bamboo skewers should be soaked in cold water for 30 minutes to prevent them from burning too quickly.

HANGING WIRE GRIDS Various shapes are available for holding fish, meat, and vegetables.

Drip trays, a grill basket, meat thermometer, poker, and a meat rack may also prove useful for some kinds of cookery.

A SELECTION OF NECESSARY EQUIPMENT FOR GRILLING

Countdown to Ignition

Until you are reasonably experienced at the barbecue grill, don't invite friends over unless you know them well: you'll have to learn what you are doing first.

1 Plan your shopping. Go for something easy to begin with—maybe steaks—and don't forget the aluminum foil and (very important) the fuel.

2 Plan when you are going to eat. You will need to start the fire about half an hour before you want to begin cooking—maybe less for a small wood fire, maybe more for a large charcoal fire. Starting the fire late will mean tiresome delays, but starting it too early may mean adding another half-sack of fuel before you start cooking, because the first lot has burned away.

3 Get organized. Have everything set up so that you know where it is. Ten minutes wasted while you look for the tongs can be disastrous. If it's a social occasion, make sure there is room for other people to cluster around the grill and talk to you.

4 Do any advance cooking that you can. Make the garlic bread; set the potatoes baking in the oven, if you are going to do it that way; cut up vegetables, whether for *crudités* or for cooking, and make the dips.

5 Start the fire. Check the manufacturer's instructions supplied with your grill to calculate the amount of fuel you will need. Alternatively, here is a rough guide. Spread a layer at least 1½ inches deep across the floor of the grill. If you are cooking a small amount of food on a large grill, the area of coals should be at least 2 inches bigger than the area that will be covered by the food. If you are using wood, you will need more fuel—at least 2 inches—and if you are cooking larger cuts of meat, you should have extra fuel heaped at the sides of the grill to add later.

Make a mound of the fuel for lighting and if you are using wood or real charcoal, put the smaller bits at the bottom and the larger ones on top. The fuel is now ready to light. Keep the lid off the grill until the charcoal is ready for cooking.

If you think that charcoal briquettes impart a chemical taste, the oil aroma of "starter fluids" (or, worse still, waxes) will really offend your nose and your taste buds. Electric fire-starters are a much better idea as are the "chimney" starters that you prime with wadded newspaper. A gas-powered blowtorch is also clean and fairly easy to use. These are available cheaply at all good hardware stores. Start the coals in a mound, then spread them out when they are burning well. Do not cover the grill until you reach this stage.

The coals are not ready for cooking on until they are just what their name suggests—coals—with no visible flame. Charcoal and wood should be covered with a fine layer of gray-white ash: if there is still any black showing on charcoal (including briquettes), the fire is not ready. At night, there should be an even red glow with just the suspicion of a blue haze around the coals.

For gas grills, remove the lid and ignite the burners. Gently close the lid and, following the manufacturer's instructions, leave the grill to heat up to cooking temperature.

While you are cooking, you can throw any or all of the following onto the coals for flavor:
Soaked wood chips
Garlic cloves
Bay leaves
Onion skins
Salt
Peppercorns
Dried or fresh herbs (such as sage, oregano, rosemary).

Vigilance

*Keep a constant eye on your fire to make sure that it is
staying at the heat required.*

CHARCOAL Regulate the temperature by moving the food
toward, or away from, the fire. Alternatively, move the
coals around. To increase the heat, push the coals closer
together. To reduce the heat, spread them out a little and
partly close the vents.

If you require the grill to stay hot for more than an hour,
you will need to add more charcoal. Either add pieces
around the edges or, once the first batch is lit, light a
second batch in an old metal roasting pan and transfer
the hot coals to the grill with metal tongs. Do not pile
cold charcoal on top of the fire: this will only deaden it.

GAS Regulate the temperature by adjusting the gas flow
or by moving the food toward or away from the heat.

Sizzling Skills

GRILLING Probably the simplest method of cooking, this
is carried out by placing food within a few inches of the
direct heat of a fire so it cooks by conduction, searing the

food on the outside to seal the juices inside, the crusty
brown surface giving the recognizable "grilled" flavor.
Once seared, the food can be moved to the cooler edges
of the grill to finish cooking.

BARBECUING To most of us this simply means cooking on
a grill in the open air. However, to real enthusiasts, true
barbecuing is slow smoking over a low fire, with the lid on
and the coals spread around the edges only (or the gas
turned off in the area directly under the food), to give a
really tender result with a smoky flavor. The top of the
food is cooked by heat reflected from the inside of the
metal lid. This way, it is possible to use tougher cuts of
meat that normally have plenty of flavor.

SKILLET OR PAN COOKING Use skillets, pans, and woks
on the grill, just as you would when using a conventional
stove.

ROTISSERIE COOKING Many portable and larger grills
incorporate a spit on which you can roast fish, poultry,

and joints of meat. Follow the manufacturer's instructions when using these.

Cooking Tips

Before you begin any cooking on the grill, it is a good idea to brush the cooking grid lightly with oil; this will help to prevent the food from sticking to the grids, which can be very difficult to clean off later.

Leave room between items of food, sufficient to turn and move them to hotter or cooler areas. When using skewers, leave a small amount of space between the food pieces, so they will cook evenly.

Check the food frequently while it is cooking, particularly when grilling small, tender pieces. However, if you are slow "smoking" a large piece of food with the lid on, resist the temptation to peek too frequently. Each time the lid is opened some heat will be lost. To compensate, add a little extra to the total cooking time.

Flare-ups

Flare-ups are caused by fat, juices, and marinades dripping onto the fire. Sudden flames leap up at the food to blacken it, giving it a nasty taste. Use a spray bottle of cold water to douse any flames that appear, and leave it handy beside the grill during cooking.

Cleaning Up

Any food left stuck to the grids after a barbecue could cause a health hazard and will definitely affect the taste of your next grilled meal.

Cleaning up is best done while the grill is still hot. Brush the cooking grid with a wire brush, allowing the food residues to fall into the dying fire. Should the food refuse to burn off the cooking grid, use hot soapy water and a scouring pad. Once the grill has cooled completely, brush out and dispose of the ashes.

Gas grills will need their cooking grids and heat plates or bars scraped of old food. Lava rocks can be used over and over again, but they will last longer if they are washed in hot soapy water occasionally, to remove grease and grime.

Be Safe

Follow the manufacturer's instructions for lighting, using, and cleaning the grill.

Before cooking make sure you keep all food covered, cool, and out of the sun.

Thaw frozen food completely before cooking.

Position the grill on a solid, level surface, out of high wind, and away from tree branches, bushes, wooden fences, and outbuildings.

Disposable and portable models should be placed on a heatproof surface (bricks are good) or on the ground.

Never light a charcoal grill with gasoline, denatured alcohol, or paraffin. It is dangerous and will taint and spoil the food.

Open the lid of a gas grill before lighting it.

Never apply lighting fluid, gel, or firelighters to a charcoal grill which has already been lit.

In the unlikely event that the grill catches fire, have handy a fire extinguisher or a bucket of sand or garden soil to throw over it.

Do not attempt to move a grill which has already been lit.

Never leave a grill unattended and do not allow children or animals near it.

Leave the grill to cool completely before moving it or packing it away.

Recipe Notes

All spoon measurements are level unless otherwise stated.

Ingredients are conveniently listed in the order in which they are used.

Cooking times are approximate and should be used as a guide only. They will vary according to the starting temperature of the food and its thickness as well as the heat of the grill.

Chapter
2

Soak It & Savor It
Marinades, basting, and sauces

Much of the characteristic flavor of barbecued food comes from the delicious tastes imparted by the marinades in which the meats are soaked, and the bastes used to keep the food moist while cooking. The choice of marinade helps focus the accompaniments. Try the rich Mediterranean-inspired Red Wine Marinade with barbecued eggplants and salads rich in tomatoes and olives to conjure up images of warm, scented nights in the olive groves. Alternatively, serve tandoori-marinated meats with perfumed rice, mango salsa, and naan bread to evoke the spiced street food of an Indian bazaar.

A MARINADE IS INTENDED TO FLAVOR AND (USUALLY) TO TENDERIZE MEAT BEFORE IT IS COOKED, WHILE A BASTING SAUCE IS INTENDED TO KEEP IT MOIST WHILE IT IS COOKING. SOMETIMES, MARINATING AND BASTING MAY BE DONE WITH THE SAME SAUCE, WHEREAS OTHER DISHES HAVE ONE SAUCE THAT IS MADE FOR A MARINADE AND ANOTHER FOR BASTING.

Soaking in almost any liquid—even water—will tenderize meat, especially if you leave it overnight; but some liquids add more flavor than others, and some actually have a chemical action which helps to tenderize tough cuts. Papaya (papain) juice is probably the most powerful of these tenderizers, and indeed the enzyme extracted from papaya was the first commercially popular meat tenderizer. Fresh pineapple juice is almost as effective.

The trouble with commercial tenderizers, as well as with soaking in papaya or pineapple marinades for too long, is that they can be altogether *too* effective: the meat is reduced to pulp. In general, a commercial tenderizer (which is only a tenderizer, and does nothing for flavor) should not be used for more than an hour or two, and a papaya or pineapple tenderizer should only be used for two to four hours. Tenderizers which use citrus juice (usually lime or lemon) can be left overnight, although more than 12 hours in a strong citrus marinade can be too much. Marinades based on beers, wines, and spirits are fine for as long as you want to leave the meat: overnight is the minimum you should consider, 24 hours is better, and two or even three days is not too long, provided everything is covered in the refrigerator.

When you leave meat in a marinade, use a glass or ceramic bowl or (easiest of all) a self-sealing plastic bag. Some stainless steel bowls will be alright. Enamel is fine if there are no chips in the finish, but iron will react with many marinades to give an unattractive metallic taste. It is inadvisable to use aluminum as it may dissolve entirely, especially if the marinade is acidic. Depending on the shape of the container, the size of the meat, and the shape of the cut, you should turn the meat in the marinade a few times in order to make sure that it is uniformly soaked. Usually, four to six turns and rearrangements are enough.

To baste, use a basting brush. Keep it clean when you are not using it, and make sure that you have somewhere clean to rest it (a plate, or a piece of aluminum foil) while you are cooking.

APPLE TARRAGON MARINADE

Apple Tarragon

*This classic combination of apple and tarragon is particularly successful
with chicken, turkey, or lamb. Marinate for between 4 and 24 hours for best results.*

Makes 2 cups

❖ 1 cup fresh apple juice or
   cider (alcoholic or
   non-alcoholic)
❖ ⅓ cup cider vinegar
❖ ¼ cup olive oil

❖ **Bunch of scallions (whole
   with tops), chopped**
❖ **3 Tbsp honey**
❖ **1 Tbsp chopped fresh
   tarragon**
❖ **Salt and freshly ground
   black pepper**

Mix all the ingredients in a saucepan (do not use
aluminum pans as they react with the acid), bring to a
boil, and simmer for 20 minutes. Cool before using.

Pineapple Marinade

*Pineapple is a natural tenderizer, so is ideal for use on cheaper cuts of meat. This marinade works
especially well for pork. Marinate for 2 to 6 hours.*

Makes 2 cups

❖ 1½ cups mashed fresh
   pineapple
❖ ½ cup dry sherry

❖ **2 garlic cloves, crushed**
❖ **½ Tbsp chopped fresh
   rosemary**
❖ **2 Tbsp raw brown sugar
   or honey, optional**

Mix the first four ingredients together. If you have a very
sweet tooth, add the 2 tablespoons of honey or raw
brown sugar.

Cooked Red Wine Marinade

*Simmering the vegetables, spices, and herbs in the wine mellows their flavors and draws
them into the wine (which is also concentrated by the simmering), so giving a marinade
that has a richer, more well-rounded flavor than an uncooked marinade.*

Makes 1½ cups

* 4 Tbsp olive oil
* 1 small onion, chopped
* 2 garlic cloves, chopped
* 1 small carrot, chopped
* 1 celery stick, chopped

* 1¾ cups medium-bodied red wine
* 4 Tbsp red wine vinegar
* 6 juniper berries, crushed
* 6 black peppercorns, crushed
* 1 bouquet garni

Heat half the oil in a saucepan, add the onion, garlic, carrot, and celery and cook until soft but not browned. Add the wine, wine vinegar, juniper berries, peppercorns, and bouquet garni. Bring to a boil then simmer for 15 to 20 minutes until the vegetables are tender. Add the remaining oil, cover, and leave to cool before using.

White Wine Marinade

*Lighter than a red wine marinade, this recipe is suitable for lamb,
chicken, turkey, and pork as well as farmed pigeon and rabbit, young
partridge and pheasant, when you want a more robust dish.*

Makes about 1¼ cups

* 2 Tbsp mild olive oil
* 1 shallot, finely chopped
* 1 carrot, finely chopped
* 2 juniper berries, crushed
* 2 black peppercorns, crushed

* 1 sprig of celery leaves, chopped
* 2 parsley sprigs
* 1 bay leaf, torn
* 1 sprig of thyme
* 1 slice of lemon
* About 1¼ cups medium-bodied dry white wine

Put all the ingredients into a bowl and stir. If the meat is not covered by the marinade, add some more wine.

Beer Marinade

*Ideally, use beer you can really taste, such as Guinness or any other strong-
flavored beer. This marinade is ideal for beef or game, such as venison.*

Makes 2 cups

* 1½ cups beer
* 2 Tbsp cider or wine vinegar
* ½ cup olive oil

* 1 small onion, thinly sliced
* 2 garlic cloves, finely chopped
* Salt and freshly ground black pepper

Mix all the ingredients together. Marinate for 8 to 48 hours.

Tandoori Marinade

This is an authentic-tasting tandoori marinade for skinned chicken portions, cubes of lamb, raw jumbo shrimp peeled but with the heads left on, or firm-fleshed fish. Marinate for 4 to 24 hours

Makes about 2 cups

- 1 onion, coarsely chopped
- 4 large garlic cloves
- 1 oz fresh ginger
- 4 Tbsp lemon juice
- 1 cup plain yogurt
- 4 Tbsp sunflower oil
- 1 Tbsp ground turmeric

- 1 Tbsp ground coriander
- 1 tsp ground cumin
- ½ tsp ground cinnamon
- ½ tsp grated nutmeg
- ½ tsp freshly ground black pepper
- ¼ tsp ground cloves
- ¼ tsp ground chiles or cayenne pepper

Put the onion, garlic, and ginger into a blender and process until chopped. Add the remaining ingredients and mix until smooth.

Pineapple Sauce

This tangy sauce is great with chicken and pork. Serve with wild rice or mixed grains and a green salad.

Makes 1 cup

- 1 cup canned crushed pineapple

- 2 tsp cornstarch
- 3 Tbsp honey
- 2 Tbsp soy sauce
- 2 Tbsp cider vinegar

Combine the pineapple and the cornstarch in a saucepan (do not use aluminum as it will react with the acid) and add the other ingredients. Heat for about 5 minutes, stirring constantly until the sauce comes to a boil and thickens. Leave to cool before using.

Apricot-Ginger Sauce

This may be a little sweet for some tastes. Substituting fresh apricots, which are then liquidized in a food processor, results in a remarkable sauce! It requires no cooking; just mix and use.

Makes 1 cup

- ¾ cup apricot preserve
- 2 Tbsp cider vinegar
- 2 Tbsp melted unsalted butter
- 1 tsp finely chopped fresh ginger

Mix all the ingredients together. Use as a mop in the last 10 minutes of cooking or simply serve as a sauce.

BEST BARBECUE SAUCE AND APRICOT-GINGER SAUCE

Best Barbecue Sauce

You can vastly improve the flavor of barbecued spare ribs and such by making up your own barbecue sauces instead of using commercial bottled sauce. Remember two things. First, thin sauces make better marinades. Second, both tomato and sugar will burn if they are applied too early. Sweet, thick barbecue sauces should only be applied just before the meat has finished cooking, about 10 to 15 minutes before it is ready.

Makes 2 cups

- 1¼ cups fresh tomato sauce
- ⅓ cup vinegar
- ⅓ cup brown sugar
- 1 medium onion, chopped
- 1 to 4 garlic cloves, finely chopped
- 1 Tbsp chili powder
- 2 Tbsp mild mustard

Mix all the ingredients in a saucepan (do not use aluminum pans as they react with acid), bring to a boil, and simmer for 5 minutes.

Chapter

3

Magically Grilled Meats

What could be more inviting than the aroma of sizzling meats fresh off the grill? Most meats cook so quickly that they are best marinated for extra flavor. The selection here includes Asian soy-based marinades, spicy Mexican marinades with fiery chiles, sweet and fruity marinades made from apples or oranges, and a gentle lemon and garlic-based marinade from Greece.

It is best to trim the fat off your meat before cooking. As well as reducing calories, you reduce the risk of troublesome flare-ups that can char the meat and spoil the delicate flavors imparted by the marinades.

Spiced Barbecued Beef Ribs

The traditional accompaniments to this Korean-inspired recipe are rice and a selection of salads.
Beef or pork spareribs can be used instead of beef short ribs.

Serves 4
Preparation time: 10 minutes
Marinating time: 3 to 4 hours
Cooking time: 30 minutes

❖ 2 lb beef short ribs, cut
   into 3-inch lengths
❖ 1 Tbsp crushed toasted
   sesame seeds (see tip
   below)
❖ 4 Tbsp soy sauce

❖ 4 scallions, white parts
   only, sliced and crushed
❖ 3 garlic cloves, crushed
   and finely chopped
❖ 1½ Tbsp sesame oil
❖ 1-inch piece of fresh
   ginger, shredded
❖ 2 tsp sugar
❖ Freshly ground black
   pepper
❖ Toasted sesame seeds,
   to taste

Tip
Toast the sesame seeds in a dry pan until they begin to pop–in about 1 minute. Crush lightly with a pestle and mortar.

Using a sharp knife, cut the meaty sides of the ribs through to the bone in a lattice pattern. This lets the marinade penetrate, tenderizes the meat, and hastens cooking. Place the ribs in a dish.

Mix together the remaining ingredients, except the garnish, and pour over the meat. Stir to mix, then cover and leave for at least 3 to 4 hours, preferably overnight.

Preheat the barbecue. Lift the meat from the marinade. Grill the beef, brushing occasionally with the marinade, until it is a rich golden brown. This should take approximately 12 to 15 minutes on each side. Serve hot, sprinkled with sesame seeds.

LEFT: SPICED BARBECUED BEEF RIBS

Yucatecan Steak

Barbecuing a handful of scallions alongside whatever else is on the grill is authentically Mexican.
Cut the onions on the diagonal, as otherwise the long strands can stick in the throat. The cabbage relish is even better
prepared a day ahead. Accompany with black beans, corn tortillas, salsa, and wedges of lime and orange.

Serves 4
Preparation time: 20 minutes
Marinating time: 30 minutes
Cooking time: 6 to 10 minutes

❖ 4 thin steaks, beef, pork,
   or venison
❖ 3 garlic cloves, chopped
❖ 2 Tbsp tequila
❖ 2 Tbsp mild red chili
   powder
❖ 2 Tbsp chopped fresh
   cilantro
❖ Juice of ½ orange
❖ Juice of 2 or more limes

❖ 6 to 10 scallions, trimmed
❖ 6 Tbsp olive oil
❖ ½ onion, shredded
❖ Salt, to taste
❖ ½ white or green
   cabbage, thinly sliced
❖ Pinch of dried oregano
❖ ½ green chile, thinly
   sliced

Combine the steaks with the garlic, tequila, chili powder, cilantro, orange juice, 1 tablespoon lime juice, scallions, half the olive oil, shredded onion, and salt to taste. Cover and leave to marinate for about 30 minutes.

Prepare the relish. Combine the cabbage with the oregano, green chile, remaining olive oil, and remaining lime juice, and salt to taste.

Preheat the grill to hot, and grill the steaks and scallions quickly until they are just cooked. Since they are thin, they need only cook 3 to 5 minutes on each side.

Slice the scallions into more easily chewable slices and serve with the relish alongside the steaks.

Orange and Honey Rib Steaks

A simple, but effective marinade works wonders for rib steaks.

Serves 4 to 6
Preparation time: 15 minutes
Marinating time: 2 to 24 hours
Cooking time: 8 to 12 minutes

❖ 1¼ cups orange juice
❖ 3 Tbsp honey

❖ 2 Tbsp lemon juice
❖ 1 Tbsp soy sauce
❖ 3 Tbsp Worcestershire
   sauce
❖ 4 to 6 beef rib steaks cut
   1-inch thick

Pour the orange juice into a saucepan, add the honey, and heat gently, stirring until the honey has dissolved.

Remove from the heat and add the remaining ingredients. Leave to cool.

Pour the marinade over the rib steaks, cover, and leave for 2 hours at room temperature or in the refrigerator for 24.

Preheat the grill. Place the steaks on the hot grill and cook, turning and basting with the marinade occasionally, until well browned on the outside but still pink and juicy inside, 8 to 12 minutes. Cook for a few minutes longer for well done, taking care not to char the outside.

Beef Teriyaki

Serve this beef with rice and vegetables cooked Japanese style and accompanied by prepared Teriyaki sauce. If pressed for time, commercial sauce can be quite good, especially if pepped up with a little chopped garlic. Alternatively, serve as a starter for up to twelve people.

Serves 4 to 6
Preparation time: 20 minutes
Cooking time: 10 to 15 minutes

❖ 2 to 3 lbs round or chuck
   steak, in a single slice, at
   least 1-inch thick and
   frozen for 1 hour

For the Teriyaki Sauce
❖ 1 cup soy sauce
❖ ⅔ cup cooking sake
   (mirin) or dry sherry
❖ ⅓ cup vinegar
❖ 2 Tbsp sesame oil
❖ 1 tsp finely chopped
   fresh ginger
❖ Salt and freshly ground
   black pepper

While the meat is semi-frozen, cut it across the grain into long strips as thin as possible: ⅛-inch thick is about right.

Mix together all the ingredients for the sauce and set aside while you cook the meat.

Preheat a hot grill. Cook the meat for 3 to 4 minutes until it is browned but not dried out. Serve with the sauce.

Korean Broiled Beef

Known as Pulgogi, *this is one of the most popular Korean dishes.* Pulgogi *is also the name of the domed-shape metal hotplate that is put on a table-top burner for cooking the beef. Serve with rice sprinkled with sesame seeds, and a cucumber and red chile salad.*

Serves 4
Preparation time: 10 minutes
Marinating time: 1 hour
Cooking time: 10 minutes

* 4 scallions, coarsely chopped
* 3 large garlic cloves, crushed and finely chopped
* 1 Tbsp crushed toasted sesame seeds (see page 23)
* 3 Tbsp soy sauce
* 2 tsp cooking sake (mirin) or dry sherry
* 1 Tbsp sesame oil
* 2 Tbsp sugar
* Freshly ground black pepper
* 1¼ pounds filet mignon, sirloin, or round steak, frozen for 1 hour
* Vegetable oil, for brushing

Mix together the scallions, garlic, sesame seeds, soy sauce, sake or sherry, sesame oil, sugar, 2 tablespoons water, and plenty of black pepper.

Cut the beef crossways into large ¼-inch thick slices. Lay in a shallow dish. Pour over the scallion mixture, cover, and leave to marinate for 1 hour.

Preheat the grill. Lightly oil the grill rack and cook the beef in batches in a single layer for about 1 minute on each side, until browned on the outside but still pink inside.

Barbecued Steak and Shiitake Mushrooms with Red Chili-garlic Butter

This is delicious! The earthy, smoky scent of the fire perfumes the fungi with its enticing aroma and flavor.

Serves 4
Preparation time: 45 minutes
Marinating time: 30 minutes
Cooking time: 22 to 25 minutes

- ❖ **12 large shiitake mushrooms**
- ❖ **5 Tbsp olive oil**
- ❖ **8 large garlic cloves, chopped**
- ❖ **2 Tbsp lemon juice**
- ❖ **Salt and freshly ground black pepper, to taste**
- ❖ **1 tsp chopped fresh thyme**
- ❖ **2½ lb fillet or fillet tail steak**
- ❖ **3 Tbsp red wine**

For the Red Chili-garlic Butter
- ❖ **6 Tbsp (¾ stick) unsalted butter, softened**
- ❖ **3 to 4 large garlic cloves, chopped**
- ❖ **1 tsp mild red chili powder, or more, to taste**
- ❖ **1 tsp paprika**
- ❖ **¼ tsp ground cumin, or to taste**
- ❖ **½ tsp crushed or chopped fresh oregano or lime leaves**
- ❖ **Juice of ¼ lime or lemon**
- ❖ **Salt**

Marinate the mushrooms in half the olive oil, half the garlic, the lemon juice, some salt and pepper, and half the thyme. Toss the steak in the remaining olive oil, garlic, and thyme, and add the red wine. Cover and leave both to marinate for at least 30 minutes while you start the barbecue.

Combine the ingredients for Red Chili-garlic Butter and mix well. Set aside.

Barbecue the steak for about 8 minutes on each side for rare to medium rare, then remove from the grill, and keep warm while you grill the mushrooms. This rest will relax the meat fibers for a more tender dish.

Cook the mushrooms for about 3 minutes on each side until the inside is juicy and the outside is nicely browned. If the shiitakes are small and threaten to fall through the barbecue grid, thread them onto skewers.

Slice the steak about ¾ inch thick across the grain, and serve each portion with several mushrooms and a dollop of Red Chili-garlic Butter sprinkled with remaining thyme.

RIGHT: BARBECUED STEAK AND SHIITAKE MUSHROOMS

Hamburger with Horseradish-mustard Cream

*Horseradish and beef is a classic combination, and this is made
even more tangy by the addition of the whole-grain mustard. Serve in buns accompanied by a bottle of red wine.*

Serves 4
Preparation time 15 minutes
Chilling time: 1 hour
Cooking time: 5 to 7 minutes

For the Horseradish-mustard Cream
- ❖ **3 Tbsp whole-grain mustard**
- ❖ **2 Tbsp grated fresh horseradish, or horseradish sauce**
- ❖ **1 tsp honey**
- ❖ **1 cup sour cream**
- ❖ **2 Tbsp chopped parsley**

- ❖ **1¼ lb ground chuck steak**
- ❖ **1 garlic clove, crushed**
- ❖ **1½ tsp salt**
- ❖ **½ tsp freshly ground black pepper**
- ❖ **2 Tbsp chopped parsley**
- ❖ **1 Tbsp olive oil**

Mix the mustard, horseradish, and honey. Stir in the sour cream and parsley. Cover and chill for at least an hour, removing from the refrigerator half an hour before serving.

In a bowl, combine the chuck, garlic, salt, pepper, parsley, and olive oil. Divide the mixture into four and shape into patties ¾- to 1-inch thick. Cook over a preheated hot grill until well browned on the outside, and cooked but moist on the inside, 5 to 7 minutes for medium rare; cook for 1 to 2 minutes longer for well done. Serve the hamburgers with a generous helping of the Horseradish-mustard Cream and plenty of crisp iceberg lettuce or watercress.

Grilled Rare Steak and Plantains with Chili-tomato Salsa

The roasted, meaty flavor of rare steak cooked over the coals is enhanced by a dab of smoky Chili-tomato Salsa. Ripe plantains, browned over the coals as well, provide a sweet, starchy sidenote. A bed of greens is refreshing next to the rich meat and plantains.

Serves 4
Preparation time: 20 minutes
Cooking time: 12 to 14 minutes

◈ 4 tender steaks such as rib-eye or top sirloin, about 6 oz each
◈ 3 cloves garlic, chopped
◈ Salt and freshly ground black pepper
◈ 1 Tbsp olive oil
◈ 2 ripe plantains (cooking bananas), peeled and cut into halves widthways

◈ Pinch of ground cinnamon

For the Salsa
◈ 2 drops chili sauce
◈ 14 oz fresh or canned tomatoes, chopped
◈ ½ red onion, chopped
◈ Pinch of cinnamon
◈ Pinch of ground cumin
◈ 1 Tbsp chopped fresh oregano
◈ Wedges of lime and chopped fresh oregano, to taste

LEFT: GRILLED RARE STEAK AND PLANTAINS WITH CHILI-TOMATO SALSA

Rub the meat with 1 clove of chopped garlic, then sprinkle with salt and pepper. Rub with olive oil and set aside. Sprinkle the plantains with cinnamon and set aside.

To make the salsa, combine the chili sauce with the tomatoes, onion, and remaining garlic; season with the cinnamon, cumin, oregano, and salt and pepper.

Preheat the grill to hot. Cook the steaks until lightly charred on the outside, rare within. Depending on the thickness, they should take only about 3 to 4 minutes on each side.

Add the plantains to the grill and cook until lightly browned in spots, about 3 minutes on each side.

Serve each steak with half a plantain, garnished with lime wedges and fresh oregano.

Skewered Venison with Prunes

Farm-reared venison is now available year-round. It benefits from the hearty flavors of a robust marinade, in which it needs to sit overnight. Cook this dish for special guests who will really appreciate it.

Serves 4
Preparation time: 30 minutes
Marinating time: 12 hours
Cooking time: 15 to 20 minutes

◈ 2 lb boneless venison, for example, haunch or steak

◈ Red Wine Marinade (page 18)
◈ 16 thick bacon rashers
◈ 32 ready-to-eat dried, pitted prunes
◈ 16 bay leaves

Trim any small areas of fat off the venison, then cut it into chunks. Place them in a dish and pour the marinade over. Cover and chill overnight.

Cut the rinds off the bacon and cut each rasher in half. Wrap a piece of bacon around each prune. Remove the meat from the marinade. Thread the meat, wrapped prunes, and bay leaves on eight metal skewers.

Brush the kebobs all over with marinade, then cook them over a preheated medium grill for 15 to 20 minutes, turning two or three times and brushing often with the marinade. The venison may be served cooked through or pink in the middle according to personal preference.

Lamb Kebobs

These small skewers of meat known as souvlakia *are traditionally cooked over charcoal and served as a snack, often on street corners. They are excellent served with pita bread and Greek salad (see below).*

Serves 4 to 6
Preparation time: 20 minutes
Marinating time: 2 hours
Cooking time: 10 minutes

❖ 3 Tbsp olive oil
❖ 3 Tbsp freshly squeezed
   lemon juice
❖ **2 tsp dried thyme**
❖ **2 garlic cloves, crushed**
❖ **Freshly ground black
   pepper, to taste**
❖ **2¼ lb lean lamb, cut into
   1-inch cubes**
❖ **6 bay leaves**
❖ **Lemon wedges, to serve**

To make the marinade, mix together the olive oil, lemon juice, thyme, garlic, and freshly ground black pepper in a screw-top jar. Secure the lid and shake well to combine the ingredients.

Place the cubed lamb in a shallow dish. Crumble two bay leaves and sprinkle over the meat. Pour the marinade over the meat and stir to coat evenly. Cover and refrigerate for 2 hours.

Thread the remaining bay leaves onto four metal skewers, then divide the meat among them. Cook the kebobs on a hot grill for about 5 to 10 minutes, or until they are cooked through. Brush with the marinade and turn the kebobs during cooking. Serve with the lemon wedges.

Serving with Pita and Greek Salad

Heat the pita bread for 15 to 30 seconds on each side: it should puff up and make it easy to slit for filling. The traditional Greek salad filling consists of shredded white cabbage with a dressing of olive oil and lemon juice, about three parts oil to one part of lemon juice. Add a couple of slices of tomato, 1 tablespoon or so of diced cucumber, and 1 teaspoon raw chopped onion. Give your guests the option of extra green bell pepper slices, too.

Put the salad in the pita first, then strip the meat cubes off the skewer and place them with the salad in the pita. Finally, lay some bell pepper over the top and serve with wedges of lemon to squeeze over the meat.

Minted Apple Lamb Steaks

Served with caramelized apples, these lamb steaks are full of flavor.

Serves 4
Preparation time: 5 minutes
Marinating time: up to 24 hours
Cooking time: 15 to 20 minutes

❖ 6 juniper berries
❖ 2 mint sprigs
❖ Salt and freshly ground
   black pepper

❖ 6 Tbsp apple juice
❖ 4 lamb steaks, off the
   leg, about ½ to ¾ lb
   each
❖ 2 dessert apples
❖ Lemon juice
❖ 3 Tbsp brown sugar

Crush the juniper berries in a heavy pestle and mortar. Add the mint leaves (discard the stalks) and crush them lightly, then mix in plenty of seasoning, and pour in the apple juice. Place the lamb steaks in a dish and spoon the apple juice mixture over them. Cover and marinate in the refrigerator overnight or for up to 24 hours.

Just before cooking the steaks, peel and core the apples. Cut each apple into four slices and sprinkle with a little lemon juice. Preheat the grill and cook the steaks over a medium heat for 5 to 10 minutes on each side. Brush with any remaining marinade during cooking.

When the steaks have been turned, sprinkle the sugar over the apples. Turn the slices in the sugar and lemon juice, then grill them briefly until they are just beginning to brown: 1 to 2 minutes on each side is usually long enough. Top each lamb steak with slices of apple before serving.

Butterfly Lamb Chops with Basil

Olive oil, garlic, basil, and pine nuts are tell-tale signs of the Italian origins of this dish.

Serves 4
Preparation time: 10 minutes
Marinating time: 2 hours
Cooking time: 10 to 16 minutes

❖ 4 butterfly lamb chops
   (double loin chops)
❖ 1 garlic clove, chopped

❖ 1 Tbsp olive oil
❖ Handful of fresh basil
   leaves, shredded
❖ 3 Tbsp pine nuts, toasted
❖ Salt and freshly ground
   black pepper
❖ 4 lemon wedges, to
   serve

Place the chops in a dish. Sprinkle the garlic, oil, and about a quarter of the basil over the chops, then cover and chill for a couple of hours.

Meanwhile, mix the remaining basil with the pine nuts and seasoning. Preheat the grill and cook the chops over a medium heat for 5 to 8 minutes on each side, according to whether you like your chops rare or well done.

Sprinkle the basil and pine nut mixture over the cooked chops. Serve the lemon wedges with the chops so that the juice may be squeezed over before eating the meat.

31

Green Peppercorn, Mustard, and Parsley Lamb Steaks

A spicy mustard paste is spread thickly over thick lamb steaks giving them a real lift.

Serves 4
Preparation time: 10 minutes
Marinating time: 2 to 24 hours
Cooking time: 12 to 16 minutes

- 1 Tbsp green peppercorns, finely chopped
- 4 Tbsp whole-grain mustard
- 3 Tbsp chopped scallion (white and green parts)
- ½ cup fresh bread crumbs
- 3 Tbsp chopped parsley
- ¼ tsp cayenne pepper
- 1 to 1½ Tbsp corn oil
- 4 lamb steaks, 1-inch thick

Put the peppercorns, mustard, scallions, bread crumbs, parsley, and cayenne pepper in a bowl and stir together thoroughly. Stir in the oil a drop at a time—sufficient to make a thick paste.

Spread the paste on both sides of the lamb steaks, place in a dish, cover, and leave for a minimum of 2 hours at room temperature, or refrigerated for up to 24 hours.

Preheat the grill to medium and cook the steaks for 6 to 8 minutes on each side, depending on whether you like your lamb slightly pink or well done.

Quick Jerk Pork Chops

*This dish can be whipped up in no time. The same rub can be used with
lamb chops, chicken breasts, or rib steaks. Serve with tomato and cucumber salad and
some coconut rice, and you've got a real taste of the tropics.*

Serves 4
Preparation time: 15 minutes
**Marinating time: 1 hour or
    more**
Cooking time: 30 to 35 minutes

❖ **3 Tbsp stemmed,
    seeded, and chopped
    hot peppers**
❖ **¼ cup fresh allspice
    berries or 3 Tbsp
    powdered allspice**
❖ **3 Tbsp lime juice**
❖ **2 Tbsp chopped scallion**
❖ **1 tsp hot pepper sauce**
❖ **1 tsp ground cinnamon**
❖ **1 tsp ground nutmeg**
❖ **4 pork chops, 1-inch
    thick**

In a food processor or blender, process the hot peppers, allspice, lime juice, scallion, hot pepper sauce, cinnamon, and nutmeg to make a thick paste. Rub the mixture into the chops and marinate, covered, in the refrigerator for 1 hour or longer.

Preheat the grill to hot. Grill the chops until done, 30 to 35 minutes. The seasonings will cause the chops to char on the outside.

Pork 'n' Pepper Kebobs

These tasty kebobs need no marinating so are ideal for an impromptu cookout supper.

Serves 4
Preparation time: 15 minutes
Cooking time: 30 to 35 minutes

❖ **2 lb lean boneless pork**
❖ **2 red bell peppers**
❖ **2 green bell peppers**
❖ **2 Tbsp vegetable oil**
❖ **1 Tbsp dried sage**
❖ **2 Tbsp medium sherry**
❖ **Salt and freshly ground
    black pepper**

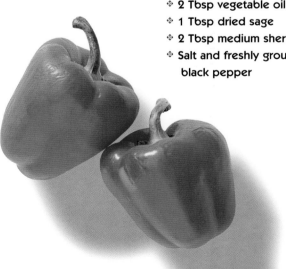

Cut the pork into 1-inch cubes. Halve the red and green bell peppers, remove their seeds and stalk, and then cut them into 1-inch squares.

Thread the meat and peppers on four metal skewers. Mix the oil, sage, sherry, and plenty of seasoning, then brush this all over the kebobs. Preheat the grill to medium and cook the kebobs, if possible with the lid on, for 30 to 35 minutes. Turn the kebobs twice and brush with any remaining oil and sherry mixture. The meat should be evenly browned and cooked through.

Coriander Pork Chops

These chops are rubbed in spices and lemon rind, and are left to absorb the flavors.
Serve with a bulgar salad full of fresh cilantro, tomatoes, and olives.

Serves 4
Preparation time: 10 minutes
Marinating time: 4 to 24 hours
Cooking time: 30 minutes

❖ 4 pork loin chops, about
  1-inch thick
❖ 3 coriander seeds,
  coarsely crushed

❖ 1 garlic clove, chopped
❖ 1 tsp grated lemon rind
❖ Salt and freshly ground
  black pepper
❖ 2 Tbsp sunflower oil
❖ 4 Tbsp thick, plain yogurt,
  to serve
❖ 2 scallions, chopped,
  to serve

Trim the rind off the chops and cut into the fat in a few places. Mix the coriander, garlic, and lemon rind, and season well.

Brush the chops all over with oil, then rub the coriander mixture over both sides of them. Place in a dish, cover, and leave to marinate in the refrigerator for several hours or overnight.

Preheat the grill to a medium heat, then cook the chops, turning once or twice, for about 30 minutes, or until they are cooked through. Top each chop with some yogurt and sprinkle with the chopped scallion before serving.

Pumpkin, Bacon, and Tomato Skewers

A light but very tasty starter of orange pumpkin and bacon, which is always a winning combination,
combined with tomatoes and Parmesan cheese. Serve on a bed of rice to make a slightly more substantial dish, but a bed of
dressed salad leaves is all that is really necessary. This also makes an excellent light lunch for two.

Serves 4 as an appetizer,
2 as a main course
Preparation time: 15 minutes
Marinating time: 30 minutes
Cooking time: 8 to 10 minutes

For the Marinade
- 3 Tbsp extra virgin
  olive oil
- 1 garlic clove, crushed
- 1 Tbsp chopped fresh
  rosemary
- Salt and freshly ground
  pepper
- 1 tsp balsamic vinegar

For the Skewers
- Three ³/₄-inch slices
  orange pumpkin, seeded
  and peeled
- 8 oz side of rindless
  bacon or 6 rashers of
  thick bacon
- 16 small tomatoes
  (baby plums are ideal)
- 2 to 3 Tbsp freshly grated
  Parmesan cheese
- Dressed salad leaves,
  to serve

Mix all the ingredients for the marinade together in a shallow dish. Cut the pumpkin into ¹/₂-inch pieces, then add to the dish, tossing it in the marinade. Cover and leave for at least 30 minutes.

Preheat the grill to medium. Cut the side of bacon into squares or stretch the bacon rashers before cutting them in half lengthways, and rolling them up. Thread the pumpkin, bacon, and tomatoes onto thin metal skewers, then brush with any remaining marinade. Grill for 6 to 8 minutes, turning occasionally, until the pumpkin is tender and the bacon browned.

Scatter the grated cheese over the skewers as soon as they are cooked, so that it melts. Serve the skewers on a bed of dressed salad leaves.

Mustard-glazed Smoked Sausage

*The smoked sausage can be replaced with your favorite thick,
cooked sausages, cut into chunks.*

Serves 4
Preparation time: 15 minutes
**Marinating time: 30 to 60
minutes**
Cooking time: 10 minutes

* 1½ lb smoked sausage,
  cut into 1-inch lengths
* 8 closed cup mushrooms

* 1 large yellow bell
  pepper, seeded and cut
  into 1-inch squares
* 2 Tbsp corn oil
* 2 Tbsp whole-grain
  mustard
* 1 Tbsp chopped fresh
  thyme
* 1 tsp wine vinegar

Thread the sausage pieces, mushrooms, and pepper alternately onto metal skewers. Mix the remaining ingredients together and brush the mixture all over the kebobs. Cover and allow to stand for ½ to 1 hour.

Preheat the grill to medium hot. Arrange the kebobs on the grill and cook for about 10 minutes or until golden brown and hot throughout. Turn occasionally and baste with any remaining mustard glaze while cooking. Serve immediately.

Chapter 4

Poultry with Pizazz

Everyone loves chicken, and the smoky flavor of grilled chicken is sensational. Chicken is quick to cook, and all the recipes here add flavor without being labor-intensive. Turkey, duck, and even quail work well on the grill, so they are included here, too. Make sure that the poultry is cooked through; the juices should run clear with no sign of pinkness in the meat.

For a quicker cookout, part-cook the chicken in a 400°F oven for 20 to 30 minutes, then simply finish on the grill. This speeds things up when cooking for a hungry crowd.

Lemon Chicken

Boneless chicken thighs work well in this recipe, too, with the lemon inside.
Serve with a couscous and tomato salad, sprinkled with crushed mixed peppercorns, and garnished with parsley.

Serves 6
Preparation time: 15 minutes
Marinating time: 2 hours
Cooking time: 25 minutes

❖ 2 lemons
❖ 6 part-boned chicken
  breasts, skin left on

❖ 3 Tbsp olive oil
❖ 2 Tbsp clear honey
❖ 2 Tbsp mustard, such as
  whole-grain or Dijon
❖ Salt and freshly ground
  black pepper

Finely grate the rind of one lemon, then squeeze out its juice. Cut the second lemon into thin slices, discarding the ends. Cut the chicken breasts lengthways, to form a

deep "pocket" (see picture). Carefully open the pocket and insert two lemon slices.

In a large bowl, whisk together the oil, honey, mustard, seasoning, lemon rind, and juice. Add the chicken pieces, turning to coat them well. Cover and allow to marinate for up to 2 hours, turning once or twice.

Preheat the grill to medium hot. Arrange the chicken on the grill and cook, turning occasionally, for about 25 minutes, or until golden brown and cooked through.

Mediterranean Chicken Skewers

The marinade of sun-dried and fresh tomatoes, olive oil, and herbs gives
the chicken a wonderfully warm flavor. Serve with Italian bread.

Serves 6
Preparation time: 10 minutes
Marinating time: 2 to 12 hours
Cooking time: 10 minutes

❖ 1 cup sun-dried tomatoes
❖ 2 fresh, ripe tomatoes
❖ ½ cup olive oil

❖ ½ cup roughly chopped
  fresh basil leaves or
  parsley
❖ Salt and freshly ground
  black pepper
❖ 6 large boneless, skinless
  chicken breasts, cut into
  cubes

Put the sun-dried and fresh tomatoes into a blender and add the oil, herbs, and seasoning. Process until smooth.

Put the chicken into a bowl and add the tomato mixture. Stir until well coated. Cover and allow to stand for about 2 hours at room temperature, or refrigerated for up to 12 hours, turning occasionally, if possible.

Thread the chicken onto metal skewers. Preheat the grill to medium hot and cook the skewers for about 10 minutes, turning frequently, and basting with any remaining marinade until cooked through.

Chicken with Avocado

The fresh, creamy avocado mixture complements the slightly spicy, full-flavored barbecued chicken.

Serves 4
Preparation time: 10 minutes
Cooking time: 45 to 50 minutes

- **4 chicken quarters**
- **1½ tsp chili powder**
- **1 tsp chopped thyme**
- **Salt and freshly ground black pepper**

- **1 Tbsp peanut oil**

For the Avocado mix
- **2 avocados**
- **4 tomatoes, diced**
- **2 scallions, chopped**
- **4 Tbsp sour cream**

Trim the leg and wing ends off the chicken if necessary and cut away any flaps of skin or fat. Mix the chili powder, thyme, and plenty of seasoning. Brush the chicken quarters with the peanut oil, then rub the seasoning mixture all over them.

Cook the chicken over a drip tray, with the lid on the barbecue. Allow about 45 to 50 minutes, turning once or twice, until the chicken is golden and crisp all over. Check that the meat is cooked through by piercing it at the thickest part with the point of a knife. If there is any sign of pink juices, cook the chicken a little longer.

Halve, peel, and slice the avocados, then mix them with the tomatoes and scallions. Pile this mixture next to the chicken on plates and top each portion with some sour cream.

Chicken Tikka

"Tikka" is Hindi for cutlet or pieces and Chicken Tikka is a traditional Hindi dish which has a truly authentic flavor when cooked on a barbecue. Cook extra and use in sandwiches with crisp iceberg lettuce and cucumber.

Serves 4

Preparation time: 15 minutes

Marinating time: 12 to 48 hours

Cooking time: 20 to 25 minutes

- 2 Tbsp grated fresh ginger
- 3 large garlic cloves
- 1 small onion, grated

- ½ tsp turmeric
- 1 Tbsp ground coriander
- 1 Tbsp ground cumin
- 4 Tbsp plain yogurt
- 2 Tbsp lemon juice
- Salt and freshly ground black pepper
- 4 large boneless chicken breasts

Mix the ginger, garlic, onion, turmeric, coriander, and cumin. Stir in the yogurt and lemon to make a paste, then add seasoning.

Remove the skin from the chicken and cut each breast into six pieces. Place the chicken pieces in a bowl and pour the spice mixture over them. Mix thoroughly, cover, and chill overnight or for up to two days (the chicken must be absolutely fresh if it is to be marinated for this long).

Thread the chicken on four metal skewers and cook on a preheated hot grill, turning often, for 20 to 25 minutes. The chicken should be very well browned and cooked through.

Garlicky Chicken

Ideal for garlic lovers! This works well using chicken thighs, too.

Serves 6

Preparation time: 20 minutes

Marinating time: 2 to 12 hours

Cooking time: 25 minutes

- 6 large garlic cloves
- 6 part-boned chicken breasts, skin left on

- 8 Tbsp (1 stick) salted butter
- 2 tsp finely grated lemon rind
- 2 Tbsp finely chopped parsley
- Salt and freshly ground black pepper

Cut each garlic clove into thin slices. Carefully lifting one side of the skin on each chicken breast, insert the garlic slices and smooth the skin back into place.
In a small pan, melt the butter and stir in the lemon rind, parsley, and a little seasoning. Brush the mixture all over the chicken. Cover and allow to stand for up to 2 hours at room temperature or refrigerate for up to 12 hours.

Preheat the grill to medium hot. Arrange the chicken on the grill and cook for about 25 minutes, turning occasionally, until golden brown and cooked through.

Grilled Chicken with Spiced Yogurt

*Chicken legs are used in this recipe, but other chicken portions work
equally well. The yogurt is used not only for flavor but also to tenderize
the meat, making it more succulent and juicy.*

Serves 6
Preparation time: 10 minutes
Marinating time: 2 to 12 hours
Cooking time: 20 to 40 minutes

❖ 6 chicken legs
❖ 3 garlic cloves, crushed
❖ Salt and freshly ground
   black pepper, to taste
❖ 1 tsp paprika

❖ 1 tsp ground cinnamon
❖ Pinch of cayenne pepper
❖ Freshly squeezed juice of
   1 lemon
❖ 8 Tbsp olive oil
❖ 8 Tbsp thick yogurt
❖ Lemon wedges, to serve

Place the chicken legs in a large, shallow dish. In a
medium-size bowl, combine the garlic, salt and freshly

ground black pepper, paprika, cinnamon, cayenne pepper,
lemon juice, oil, and yogurt.

Pour the marinade over the chicken legs, stirring and
turning them to coat evenly. Cover and leave to marinate
in the refrigerator for 2 to 3 hours or overnight.

Season the chicken legs again with plenty of salt and
freshly ground black pepper. Preheat the grill to medium
hot, then place the chicken legs on an oiled rack and cook
for 20 to 40 minutes or until crisp and golden on the
outside and cooked through, turning frequently during
cooking. Serve with lemon wedges.

Chicken Satay with Peanut Dipping Sauce

*Satays are ubiquitous throughout South East Asia, and every cook
has their own favorite recipe. This is an excellent version that can be used for satays of chicken,
pork, or large shrimp. The dressing may also be used to accompany the traditional Indonesian salad,
gado gado, a mixed vegetable salad served with tofu and thin omelet. It also works well
with warm potato salads, French beans, zucchini, and cauliflower salads.*

Serves 4
Preparation time: 30 minutes
Marinating time: 2 to 12 hours
Cooking time: 20 to 25 minutes

For the Chicken satay
- ¼ cup coconut milk
- 1 Tbsp granulated brown sugar
- 1 garlic clove, finely chopped
- 2 tsp ground coriander
- 2 tsp ground cumin
- 1 tsp ground turmeric
- Squeeze of lemon juice
- 4 boneless, skinless chicken breasts
- Lime wedges, to garnish

For the Peanut Sauce
- 2 Tbsp peanut oil
- 1 onion, finely chopped
- 1 garlic clove, crushed
- Pinch of red cayenne pepper
- ¾ cup unsalted peanuts
- ¾ cup coconut milk
- 1¼ tsp soy sauce
- Juice of 1 lime
- 1 tsp granulated brown sugar
- Salt and freshly ground black pepper
- Red chile, chopped, and lime leaves, to garnish

Combine all the ingredients for the Chicken Satay, except the chicken, to make a dry paste. Cut the chicken breasts into six to eight pieces and place in the marinade. Toss to coat evenly, then cover and marinate for 2 hours at room temperature or up to 12 hours in the refrigerator.

For the Peanut Dipping Sauce, heat the oil in a skillet, add the onion, and cook for a couple of minutes. Add the garlic and cayenne pepper and continue cooking until the onion is soft and golden. Meanwhile, put the peanuts into a food processor and process to a coarse paste. Transfer the paste to a bowl and stir in the coconut milk, soy sauce, lime juice, sugar, seasoning, and nut paste, mixing well until smooth and creamy.

Preheat the grill to medium hot. Thread the chicken on four metal skewers and cook the satay for 20 to 25 minutes, turning until the chicken is thoroughly cooked through. Garnish with lime wedges. Serve with the Peanut Dipping Sauce, garnished with red chile and lime leaves.

Tip
If the dressing is made in advance it may separate: this can be rectified by heating gently and stirring in about 1 tablespoon of water.

RIGHT: CHICKEN SATAY WITH PEANUT DIPPING SAUCE

Five-spice Chicken

Five-spice powder is an authentic Chinese flavoring, usually made up of a mixture of ground star anise, anise pepper, fennel seeds, cloves, and cinnamon or cassia. This dish is delicious served with rice garnished with small shrimp and cilantro.

Serves 6
Preparation time: 10 minutes
Marinating time: 2 to 12 hours
Cooking time: 20 minutes

- 6 Tbsp soy sauce
- 3 Tbsp sesame oil
- 3 Tbsp fresh ginger sauce, or 1 Tbsp finely chopped fresh ginger
- 3 Tbsp fish sauce
- 1 Tbsp rice vinegar or sake
- 1 Tbsp five-spice powder
- 12 chicken drumsticks

In a large bowl, mix all the ingredients except the chicken. Add the chicken to the marinade turning to coat it well. Cover and allow to stand for up to 2 hours at room temperature or refrigerate for up to 12 hours.

Preheat the grill to medium hot. Arrange the chicken on the rack and cook for about 20 minutes, turning occasionally, or until crisp, golden brown, and cooked through.

RIGHT: FIVE-SPICE CHICKEN

Chicken with Pecans and Herbs

Little parcels of nut-and-herb flavored chicken. This stuffing is also good used under the skin of chicken breasts.

Serves 6
Preparation time: 25 minutes
Marinating time: 2 to 12 hours
Cooking time: 20 minutes

- 4 Tbsp (½ stick) salted butter
- 1 small onion, finely chopped
- 1 cup fresh bread crumbs, plus extra if necessary
- ½ cup finely chopped pecans
- 4 Tbsp finely chopped herbs, such as parsley, thyme, and basil
- Salt and freshly ground black pepper
- Finely grated rind and juice of 1 orange
- 12 boneless chicken thighs, skin left on
- Walnut oil

Melt the butter in a pan and add the onion. Cook gently for 5 to 10 minutes or until the onion is soft and just turning golden brown. Put the bread crumbs into a bowl and stir in the pecans, herbs, and seasoning. Add the onion mixture, orange rind, and orange juice. Stir well, adding extra bread crumbs if necessary, to make a firm mixture. Leave to cool.

Using your hands, shape a small amount of the pecan stuffing into a ball and push into the cut side of each chicken thigh. Use string to tie each thigh into a package. Cover and leave to stand for up to 2 hours at room temperature or refrigerate for up to 12 hours.

Lightly brush the chicken thighs with walnut oil. Preheat the grill to medium hot, then arrange on the rack and cook for about 20 minutes, turning occasionally, or until golden brown and cooked through.

Sweet-and-sour Chicken Wings

The chicken wings are threaded onto kebob sticks
for easy turning on the barbecue. Alternatively, grill them in a hinged wire basket.
Serve with grilled yellow bell peppers.

Serves 6
Preparation time: 10 minutes
Marinating time: 2 to 12 hours
Cooking time: 20 minutes

- 1 medium onion, roughly chopped
- 2 large garlic cloves
- 1 small green bell pepper, seeded
- 4 canned pineapple rings, drained
- 3 Tbsp wine vinegar
- 2 Tbsp soy sauce
- 1½ Tbsp corn oil
- 1 Tbsp sugar
- 24 chicken wings
- Grated lemon rind, to garnish

Put all the ingredients, except the chicken and the lemon garnish, into a blender and process until smooth. Tip the mixture into a large, shallow dish. Add the chicken wings and turn them until well coated. Cover and allow to stand for up to 2 hours at room temperature or refrigerated for up to 12 hours, occasionally turning them in the marinade.

Preheat the grill to medium hot. Lift the chicken out of the marinade and thread onto eight skewers. Cook for about 20 minutes, occasionally brushing with the remaining marinade and turning them, until crisp and cooked through. Garnish with grated lemon rind and serve with grilled yellow bell peppers.

Chicken and Scallion Kebobs

These delicious kebobs are excellent served with rice and a Far Eastern-style salad, which complements the sweet and sour flavor of the chicken.

Serves 4
Preparation time: 15 minutes
Marinating time: 3 to 4 hours
Cooking time: 10 to 15 minutes

⬥ 1½ pounds skinned, boneless chicken thighs
⬥ 1 to 2 bunches large scallions, white parts only
⬥ 4 Tbsp soy sauce
⬥ 1 Tbsp sesame oil
⬥ 2 tsp sugar
⬥ 2 garlic cloves, finely chopped
⬥ ¾-inch piece of fresh ginger, grated
⬥ 1 Tbsp crushed toasted sesame seeds (see page 23), plus extra, to serve

Cut each chicken thigh into three lengths. Thread pieces of chicken and scallion alternately onto short skewers. Lay the skewers in a large, shallow dish.

Mix together the remaining ingredients, except the garnish, and pour over the skewers. Turn to coat with the sauce, cover, then leave to marinate for 3 to 4 hours in the refrigerator, turning occasionally.

Preheat the grill to medium. Lift the skewers from the marinade and cook for about 10 to 15 minutes, brushing with the remaining marinade and turning occasionally until cooked through. Serve with toasted sesame seeds.

Maple-glazed Drumsticks

The maple syrup is brushed onto the drumsticks toward the end of cooking.

Serves 6
Preparation time: 5 minutes
Marinating time: 2 to 12 hours
Cooking time: 20 to 25 minutes

- 2 Tbsp corn oil
- 2 large garlic cloves,
  finely chopped

- 2 tsp dried mixed herbs
- 1 Tbsp soy sauce
- 1 Tbsp wine vinegar
- 12 chicken drumsticks
- 4 Tbsp maple syrup

In a shallow dish, mix the oil, garlic, mixed herbs, soy sauce, and wine vinegar until well blended. Add the drumsticks and turn to coat them well. Cover and allow to stand at room temperature for up to 2 hours or refrigerated overnight, turning occasionally.

Preheat the grill to medium hot. Arrange the drumsticks on the rack and cook for about 10 minutes, turning occasionally. Brush the maple syrup over the drumsticks, and continue to cook for 10 minutes longer, or until crisp, golden brown, and cooked through.

Spice-rubbed Chicken

This spice combination gives a wonderfully warm flavor to the chicken.

Serves 6
Preparation time: 10 minutes
Marinating time: 2 to 12 hours
Cooking time: 20 minutes

- 3 Tbsp corn oil
- 1 Tbsp ground cinnamon
- 1 Tbsp ground coriander

- 1 Tbsp granulated brown
  sugar
- 1½ tsp paprika
- ¼ tsp cayenne pepper
- 1 tsp salt
- 6 boneless chicken
  breasts, skin left on

In a large bowl, mix all the ingredients except the chicken. Then, add the chicken and, with your hands, rub the spice mixture all over it. Cover and allow to stand for up to 2 hours at room temperature or refrigerated up to 12 hours.

Preheat the grill to medium hot and arrange the chicken on the oiled rack. Cook for about 20 minutes, turning frequently, or until slightly charred and cooked through. Serve each chicken breast cut diagonally into thin slices.

Spiced Rock Hen

*The spices are first toasted then mixed with garlic and rubbed over and under
the skin of the Cornish Game Hen. Choose a mild or hot curry powder, according to your taste.
The yogurt and cilantro make a fresh-tasting dressing to serve with the hen, and a cucumber and cherry
tomato salad garnished with crushed mixed peppercorn is an excellent accompaniment.*

Serves 4
Preparation time: 15 minutes
Marinating time: 1 hour
Cooking time: 25 minutes

- 2 tsp curry powder
- 2 tsp ground coriander
- 1 tsp ground cumin
- ½ tsp cayenne pepper
- 4 large garlic cloves, crushed
- 2 Cornish Game Hens, each quartered
- 4 Tbsp chopped fresh cilantro
- ½ cup plain yogurt
- Salt and freshly ground black pepper
- Corn oil
- Lemon wedges, to serve

Put the curry powder, coriander, cumin, and cayenne into a small skillet over a medium-low heat. Cook gently for 1 to 2 minutes, shaking the pan frequently, until the spices are fragrant. Put the mixture in a bowl with the garlic, and blend to a paste.

Rub the spice mixture on all sides of the hen pieces, lifting the skin to spread some underneath. Cover and allow to stand for about 1 hour.

Stir the cilantro into the yogurt and season lightly with salt and pepper. Cover and refrigerate until needed.

Season the hen pieces with salt and pepper, then brush lightly with oil. Preheat the grill to medium hot, then arrange the hen pieces on the rack and cook for about 25 minutes, turning occasionally, until deep brown and cooked through. Serve with the yogurt–cilantro dressing and lemon wedges to squeeze over.

Turkey Kebobs

Turkey kebobs are good with a salad of shredded Chinese cabbage and carrot.

Serves 4
Preparation time: 15 minutes
Marinating time: 2 to 6 hours
Cooking time: 30 minutes

- 2 lb boneless turkey breast
- 1 Tbsp chopped fresh rosemary
- Grated rind and juice of 1 orange
- 1 garlic clove, crushed
- 2 Tbsp olive oil
- Salt and freshly ground black pepper

The turkey meat should be skinned and trimmed of any small pieces of fat. Cut the meat into large chunks 2 inches in size. Place in a bowl. Add the rosemary, orange rind and juice, garlic, olive oil, and plenty of seasoning. Mix well to coat all the pieces of turkey in the marinade. Cover and refrigerate for 2 to 6 hours.

Remove the turkey from the marinade and thread the chunks onto eight metal skewers. Preheat the grill to a medium heat and cook the kebobs, brushing often with the marinade, for about 30 minutes, until cooked through. Turn the kebobs three or four times so that the turkey is well browned all over and crisped in parts.

Spiced Turkey Burgers with Sour Cream and Chive Dressing

These burgers have a mild Asian flavor. Serve them in split rolls, lightly toasted on the edge of the grill, with a garnish of lettuce, cucumber, and tomato.

Serves 8
Preparation time: 15 minutes
Marinating time: 30 to 60 minutes
Cooking time: 20 minutes

- 8 Tbsp (1 stick) salted butter
- 2 large garlic cloves, crushed or finely chopped
- 2 Tbsp curry powder
- ½ tsp cayenne pepper
- 2 lb ground turkey
- 4 Tbsp whole-grain mustard
- 4 Tbsp thick mango chutney or mashed mango
- 1 cup fresh bread crumbs
- 1 cup chopped fresh chives
- Salt and freshly ground black pepper
- 1 cup sour cream
- Corn oil

In a small skillet, melt the butter and stir in the garlic, curry powder, and cayenne. Cook over medium-low heat for 1 to 2 minutes, stirring frequently, or until the spices are fragrant. Put the turkey into a large bowl and add the spice mixture, mustard, chutney or mango, bread crumbs, ¾ cup chives, and seasoning. Mix well. Using your hands, divide the mixture into eight and shape into burgers. Cover and allow to stand for 30 to 60 minutes.

Mix together the sour cream and the remaining chives. Cover and refrigerate until required.

Preheat the grill to medium hot, then lightly brush the burgers with oil. Cook for about 10 minutes on each side, or until cooked through. Serve with the sour cream and chive dressing.

RIGHT: SPICED TURKEY BURGERS WITH SOUR CREAM AND CHIVE DRESSING

Turkey with Apricots and Bacon

*Flattened turkey breasts are spread with a fruity stuffing and rolled up.
The bacon wrapping keeps them moist and imparts a delicious flavor.*

Serves 8
Preparation time: 20 minutes
Cooking time: 12 minutes

❖ 8 turkey breast steaks, about 1-inch thick
❖ About 8 bacon rashers, rindless
❖ 1 cup fresh bread crumbs
❖ ½ cup chopped ready-to-eat dried apricots
❖ Finely grated rind of 1 lemon
❖ 4 Tbsp finely chopped parsley
❖ Salt and freshly ground black pepper
❖ 4 Tbsp (½ stick) salted butter, melted
❖ 1 medium egg, lightly beaten

Put one turkey steak between two sheets of plastic wrap. Using a rolling pin, beat and flatten the turkey steak until it is about twice its original size. Repeat with the remaining steaks. Using the flat side of a large knife, flatten and stretch the bacon rashers until they are about twice their original length.

Mix together the bread crumbs, apricots, lemon rind, and parsley. Season with salt and pepper. Stir in the melted butter and beaten egg. Divide the mixture into eight and spread one portion over each turkey steak. Starting at a long edge, roll up each turkey steak and wrap with bacon. Tie securely with string.

Preheat the grill to medium hot, then cook for about 12 minutes, turning frequently, or until the bacon is crisp and the turkey is cooked through. Leave to stand for 5 minutes before slicing into thick "pinwheels."

Duck with a Juniper Crust

*The aromatic tang of juniper goes well with duck. If you leave the
skin on, remember to cover the grill and cook the duck indirectly, high
above the coals, or over a medium-low heat, to avoid flare-ups.*

Serves 4
Preparation time: 10 minutes
Marinating time: 2 to 12 hours
Cooking time: 15 minutes

❖ 1 Tbsp juniper berries
❖ ½ tsp black peppercorns
❖ ½ tsp salt
❖ ½ tsp sugar
❖ 5 Tbsp fresh orange juice
❖ 4 boneless duck breasts
❖ Corn oil

Grind the juniper berries, peppercorns, salt, and sugar to a smooth powder (use a pestle and mortar or coffee grinder).

Pour the orange juice into a bowl and stir in the juniper mixture. Add the duck breasts and turn to coat them well.

Cover and allow to stand for up to 2 hours at room temperature or refrigerate for up to 12 hours.

Preheat the grill to medium, then lift the duck from the marinade and arrange on the rack. Cook for about 15 minutes or until crisp on the outside and slightly pink in the middle. Turn and baste frequently with the extra marinade while cooking. Cut diagonally into thin slices to serve.

RIGHT: DUCK WITH A JUNIPER CRUST

Duck Breasts with Pineapple and Bay

*Because duck is so very fatty, indirect, covered cooking is best
to avoid flare-ups.*

Serves 4
Preparation time: 30 minutes
Marinating time: 12 hours
Cooking time: 20 minutes

❖ 2 Tbsp vegetable oil
❖ 1 fresh green chile,
   seeded and sliced

❖ 4 bay leaves
❖ 4 shallots, chopped
❖ 8-oz can pineapple rings
   in syrup
❖ 4 duck breasts

Heat the oil gently in a small saucepan. Add the chile slices and bay leaves and cook gently, stirring occasionally, for 5 minutes. Stir in the shallots and cook for a further 5 minutes before pouring in the syrup from the can of pineapple rings. Slowly bring to a boil and simmer for 2 minutes, then leave the mixture to cool completely.

Place the duck breasts in a dish and pour the cooled marinade over them. Cover and chill overnight. Drain the duck breasts before cooking them. Pour the marinade into a small pan, bring to a boil, reduce the heat, and simmer the liquid for about 10 minutes, or until it is reduced to a small amount of glaze.

Preheat the grill to medium-hot and cook the duck breasts for about 10 minutes on each side, or until the skin is crisp and well browned, and the meat is cooked to your liking. Lightly grill the pineapple rings. Discard the bay leaves from the marinade and pour it over the duck before serving on a plate garnished with the pineapple rings.

Quail wrapped in Grape Leaves

*Quail are so small that they are more of an appetizer than a main dish, so you need
to cook two, or even three, quail per person. This is a traditional method of cooking quail which
infuses the bird with the richness of the bacon and the smoky flavor of the grape leaves.*

Serves 4
Preparation time: 30 minutes
Cooking time: 30 to 40 minutes

❖ 8 quail
❖ Freshly ground black
   pepper

❖ 24 strips of smoked
   Canadian bacon
❖ One 16-oz can grape
   leaves in brine, drained
   and rinsed

Wash and dry the quail, then season generously with freshly ground black pepper. Wrap three strips of bacon

around each bird, then wrap in vine leaves securing with twine. (Soaking the twine in water for 30 minutes reduces the chance of it catching fire while cooking.) The birds may be prepared ahead of time, covered, and kept refrigerated until required.

Roast the quail over a preheated medium-hot grill for about 15 to 20 minutes, turning frequently. Unless you have a very large grill you will probably have to cook the quail in two batches.

Chapter

5

Fabulous, Flaming Fish

Don't worry if you haven't been fishing and brought trout or salmon fresh to the grill; fish from the local market is fine. Whole fish, fish steaks, fish kebobs, and shellfish are all given a make over and enlivened with a variety of spices and marinades.

Do make sure that fish is opaque in the center before serving, but do not leave it on the grill too long as it soon overcooks. If in doubt, take if off the fire, leave it for a few minutes (it continues cooking once removed from grill), then check it again. If it is still slightly transparent, return to the grill for a minute or two more.

Swordfish Steaks with Fennel

Thick, firm, meaty swordfish barbecues really well, but cod, salmon, or tuna would be equally successful.

Serves 4

Preparation time: 10 minutes

Marinating time: 3 hours

Cooking time: 10 to 15 minutes

❖ **4 swordfish steaks, about 6 oz each**
❖ **⅔ cup salad oil**
❖ **⅔ cup red wine vinegar**
❖ **1 Tbsp brown sugar**
❖ **2 Tbsp light soy sauce**
❖ **¼ cup dry white wine**
❖ **1 garlic clove, crushed**
❖ **1 tsp fennel seeds**
❖ **1 head fennel, trimmed and cut into 8 pieces**
❖ **2 celery stalks, cut into strips**
❖ **1 red onion, cut into 8 pieces**
❖ **Grated rind of 1 lime**

Place the fish in a shallow dish. Mix the oil, vinegar, sugar, soy sauce, wine, garlic, and fennel seeds together.

Pour over the fish, cover, and marinate in the refrigerator for 3 hours.

Remove the fish from the marinade, and place a piece of fish in the center of four 12-inch squares of heavy-duty aluminum foil. Divide the vegetables and lime rind among the fish and wrap the foil around to form a parcel. Spoon 2 tablespoons of the marinade over each and seal completely.

Cook on a preheated hot grill until cooked through, about 10 to 15 minutes. Sprinkle with grated lime rind and serve hot with salad.

Grilled Salmon in Foil

*Salmon is always a treat and this slightly smoky, succulently
juicy recipe won't disappoint. Serve with an arugula- or watercress-based
salad, or as a sandwich wedged between slices of Italian bread.*

Serves 6
Preparation time: 10 minutes
Marinating time: 20 minutes
Cooking time: 20 to 30 minutes

- Corn oil or salted butter, to grease foil
- 2½ to 3 lb whole salmon, cleaned weight
- Juice of 1 lemon
- 1 Tbsp olive oil
- Salt and freshly ground black pepper
- 4 sprigs dill
- ¼ cup chopped fresh dill
- 4 Tbsp (½ stick) salted butter, softened
- 1 tsp Dijon mustard
- Lemon wedges, to serve

Heavy-duty aluminum foil is used as a cradle, rather than as a wrap. It should be long enough to cradle the whole fish, with extra at either end for ease in handling. Grease the foil thickly with butter (or brush it all over with olive oil) to prevent sticking, and poke holes in it with a knitting needle or something similar so that the smoke can reach the fish.

Season the fish inside and out with lemon juice, olive oil, salt, and pepper. Put four sprigs of dill in the cavity and place the fish on the foil. Cover and leave to stand for 20 minutes for the flavors to mingle.

Preheat a hot grill and place the salmon in the foil on the rack. After five minutes, *carefully* turn the fish in the foil cradle, and repeat at 5-minute intervals. The fish should be cooked in 20 to 30 minutes in total, depending on how you like your salmon.

Beat together the chopped dill, the softened butter, and the mustard. Roll the cooked fish onto the serving plate (this is easier than trying to lift it out of the foil). Serve with the flavored butter, and lemon wedges.

Thai-style Salmon

*This marinade is typical of Thai cuisine combining as it does herbs,
spices, and the tartness of lime juice. Serve with a shredded vegetable and bean sprout salad.*

Serves 4
Preparation time: 15 minutes
Marinating time: 2 hours
Cooking time: 10 to 12 minutes

- 2 garlic cloves
- 1 fresh green chile, seeded and finely chopped
- 2 Tbsp chopped fresh cilantro
- 2 Tbsp chopped fresh basil
- 2 Tbsp chopped fresh mint
- ½-inch piece fresh ginger, grated
- 4 Tbsp lime juice
- 1 Tbsp fish sauce
- 1 Tbsp sesame oil
- Freshly ground black pepper
- 4 salmon steaks, about 6 oz each, cut 1-inch thick

In a shallow dish combine together all the ingredients except the salmon. Add the fish and coat well in the marinade. Cover and leave for up to 2 hours.

Preheat the grill until the coals are hot, then cook the salmon on an oiled rack for 10 to 12 minutes turning once, or until opaque throughout. Baste from time to time with the marinade while cooking.

Almond Trout

The classic method for preparing this dish is to coat the trout with flour or bread crumbs,
then pan-fry them. This barbecue method uses just a little olive oil and paprika, and a crunchy topping of almonds
and scallions, resulting in a simpler dish with a wonderful flavor that saves a few calories, too.

Serves 4
Preparation time: 15 minutes
Cooking time: 10 to 12 minutes

For the almond topping
- 3 Tbsp (⅓ stick) salted butter
- 1 cup sliced blanched almonds
- 2 tsp grated lemon rind
- 2 tsp Worcestershire sauce
- 1½ Tbsp fresh lemon juice

- Few drops of Tabasco sauce

- 4 trout, about 1 lb each, heads removed, and filleted if the fish is firm enough to keep its shape
- 6 Tbsp olive oil
- 1 tsp salt
- ½ tsp paprika
- 6 scallions, chopped, to garnish
- 4 Tbsp chopped parsley, to garnish

To prepare the almond topping, melt the butter in a small skillet and add the almonds and lemon rind. Cook, stirring carefully, until golden. Combine with the Worcestershire sauce, lemon juice, and Tabasco sauce. Set aside.

Brush the inside of the trout with some of the olive oil and season with salt and paprika. Brush the outside of the fish with the remaining oil.

Preheat the grill to hot, then place the fish on a lightly oiled rack set 6 inches away from the coals. Cook for 5 to 8 minutes turning once. The trout should be browned on the outside while the flesh should be opaque close to the bone. Heat the almond mixture over the grill until warmed through and serve spooned over the trout.

Cod and Vegetable Kebobs

Ideal for a summer party, these kebobs make a delicious alternative to meat.

Serves 4
Preparation time: 20 minutes
Marinating time: 3 to 12 hours
Cooking time: 7 to 10 minutes

For the Marinade
- 3 Tbsp light soy sauce
- 2 garlic cloves, minced
- Few drops of Tabasco sauce
- 2 Tbsp olive oil
- 1 Tbsp cider vinegar

- 2 tsp molasses
- 1 red chile, sliced
- ⅔ cup fish broth

- 1½ lb cod fillets
- 4 small baking potatoes, quartered
- 2 red bell peppers, seeded and cut into large squares
- 12 large mushrooms
- 3 Tbsp olive oil

For the marinade, mix together the soy sauce, garlic, Tabasco sauce, olive oil, cider vinegar, molasses, red chile, and fish broth. Cut the fish into 1½- to 2-inch cubes. Pour the marinade over the fish, and marinate in the refrigerator for several hours or overnight. Precook the potatoes to shorten the barbecuing time. Either use a microwave for 4 minutes on high or boil them, quartered but with skins, until just tender, about 10 to 15 minutes.

To make the kebobs, use either metal skewers or wooden skewers that have been pre-soaked in water for 30 minutes. Then thread the fish cubes, potatoes, peppers, and mushrooms onto the skewers, alternating the ingredients. Brush the vegetables with olive oil.

Preheat the grill to hot. Cook the kebobs on a lightly oiled rack for 7 to 10 minutes, turning frequently until the fish is opaque throughout.

Calypso Cod Steaks

These Caribbean-style cod steaks have zip, thanks to the hot peppers. Salmon or firm, white-fleshed fish works well, too, but do not use salted cod in this dish.

Serves 4
Preparation time: 10 minutes
Cooking time: 8 to 12 minutes

- 2 Tbsp fresh lime juice
- 2 Tbsp olive oil
- 1½ tsp crushed garlic

- ½ to 1 tsp crushed hot pepper or 1 to 2 tsp hot pepper sauce
- 4 cod steaks, ¾-inch thick, about 6 oz each
- Strips of lime rind, to garnish

In a bowl, whisk together the lime juice, olive oil, garlic, and hot pepper or hot pepper sauce to taste.

Brush the grill rack with oil and preheat the grill to hot. Grill the fish steaks for about 4 to 6 minutes on one side, basting frequently with the sauce, then turn and cook on the other side for another 4 to 6 minutes, again basting frequently, until opaque but not overcooked. Serve garnished with lime rind.

Herring in Grape Leaves

*Grape leaves are perfect for wrapping around small, oily fish to hold
in the flavors and to prevent the fish from falling apart during cooking. This is an attractive
and unusual Greek specialty which works successfully on the grill.*

Serves 6
Preparation time: 30 minutes
Cooking time: 8 to 12 minutes

- ❖ **6 small herring, about 8 oz each, scaled and cleaned, heads removed**
- ❖ **Juice of 1 lemon**
- ❖ **Salt and freshly ground black pepper, to taste**

- ❖ **Olive oil, to drizzle**
- ❖ **3 tsp dried thyme or 4 tsp fresh thyme**
- ❖ **Packet or can of 12 vine leaves, drained and rinsed**
- ❖ **Fresh thyme sprigs, to serve**
- ❖ **Sea salt, to serve**
- ❖ **Lemon wedges, to serve**

Wash the herring under cold running water and pat dry with paper towels. Place the fish on a chopping board and sprinkle with lemon juice. Season with salt and freshly ground black pepper.

Drizzle the fish evenly with some olive oil and sprinkle with thyme. Lay the grape leaves out on the work surface and lightly brush with a little olive oil. Use two of the grape leaves to wrap around each fish, completely encasing it.

Preheat the grill to hot. Arrange the wrapped fish on a lightly oiled grill rack and cook for 4 to 6 minutes, on each side, or until the fish flakes easily and is cooked through. Transfer to a serving platter and sprinkle with fresh thyme sprigs. Serve with sea salt and plenty of lemon wedges.

Angler Fish Salmoriglio

*This Sicilian marinade is traditionally used for marinating fish that is to be barbecued.
Sicilians believe that the only way to make true* salmoriglio *is to add seawater; in the absence of this ingredient, use
sea salt for seasoning.* Salmoriglio *can also be served warm as a sauce to accompany fish.*

Serves 4
Preparation time: 20 minutes
Marinating time: 2 hours
Cooking time: 7 to 10 minutes

⬧ 1 garlic clove
⬧ 1 Tbsp finely chopped
   parsley
⬧ 1½ tsp chopped fresh
   oregano
⬧ 1 tsp chopped fresh
   rosemary

⬧ Sea salt
⬧ ¾ cup virgin olive oil,
   warmed slightly
⬧ 3 Tbsp hot water
⬧ 4 Tbsp lemon juice
⬧ Freshly ground black
   pepper
⬧ 1½ lb angler fish fillet,
   1-inch thick
⬧ 8 bay leaves

Put the garlic, herbs, and a pinch of sea salt into a mortar or bowl and pound to a paste with pestle or end of a rolling pin. Pour the oil into a warmed bowl then, using a fork, slowly pour in the hot water followed by the lemon juice, whisking constantly until thickened. Add the herb and garlic mixture, and black pepper to taste. Put the bowl over a saucepan of hot water and warm for 5 minutes, whisking occasionally. Leave to cool.

Cut the fish into 1-inch cubes and place in the bowl of cooled salmoriglio. Cover and leave to marinate for at least 2 hours.

Preheat the grill until the coals are hot, then thread the fish and bay leaves onto metal skewers, or wooden skewers that have been soaked in water for 30 minutes. Lightly cook the fish for 7 to 10 minutes turning frequently, until the fish is opaque throughout. Serve with roasted vegetables.

Grilled Shark

*This barbecue recipe is an easy and tasty way to cook shark,
or other dense-fleshed fish such as swordfish. It is delicious plain, but you
can also serve it with flavored butters (see page 75).*

Serves 4
Preparation time: 10 minutes
Marinating time: 2 hours
Cooking time: 10 to 12 minutes

⬧ 3 Tbsp fresh lemon juice
⬧ 3 Tbsp fresh lime juice
⬧ ½ tsp grated lemon rind
⬧ ½ tsp grated lime rind
⬧ ¼ cup olive oil

⬧ 3 Tbsp chopped fresh
   dill
⬧ 3 garlic cloves, finely
   chopped
⬧ Pinch of salt
⬧ 4 shark steaks, about
   6 oz each
⬧ Freshly ground black
   pepper

Combine all the ingredients, except the shark and pepper, in a dish. Place the shark steaks in the marinade, turning to coat thoroughly, and spreading the dill and garlic bits over tops of the fish. Sprinkle with freshly ground black pepper, cover, and refrigerate for about 2 hours, turning once or twice.

When the coals have stopped flaming, place the shark steaks on a lightly greased rack. Cook for about 5 to 6 minutes each side, turning once. (Total cooking time should be about 10 minutes per inch of thickness.) Baste with the extra marinade, if desired. The fish is cooked through when the flesh turns opaque, but is still juicy.

Tuna and Eggplant Kebobs

Fresh tuna is generally available from late spring to early fall and its rich,
meat-like flesh holds together well, making it the ideal fish for grilling.

Serves 4
Preparation time: 10 minutes
Marinating time: 1 hour
Cooking time: 15 minutes

- 1½ lb fresh tuna steaks,
  about 1-inch thick, cut
  into 1-inch cubes
- Grated rind and juice of
  1 lime

- 4 Tbsp olive oil
- 1 garlic clove, crushed
- 2 Tbsp chopped fresh
  oregano and parsley,
  mixed together
- Salt and freshly ground
  black pepper
- 1 long, thin, Japanese- or
  Thai-style eggplant

Place the tuna in a dish, then add the lime rind and juice,
olive oil, garlic, oregano, parsley, salt, and pepper. Stir
well, cover, and leave to marinate for at least 1 hour,
stirring once or twice.

Preheat the grill to medium and half cook the eggplant
until the skin is just starting to wrinkle. Cut into ½-inch
thick slices.

Thread the tuna and eggplant on metal skewers, or
wooden skewers soaked in water for 30 minutes, then
brush with the remaining marinade.

Preheat the grill and cook over a moderate heat for 5 to
6 minutes on each side, basting at intervals with any
remaining marinade.

Tuna with Thyme and Garlic

Perfect fish steaks for the garden or beach barbecue.
Serve with a rice salad—decorated with oregano.

Serves 4
Preparation time: 5 minutes
Marinating time: 2 to 12 hours
Cooking time: 14 to 16 minutes

❖ 2 lb fresh tuna steak
❖ 2 Tbsp chopped fresh
   thyme

❖ 6 Tbsp olive oil
❖ 2 garlic cloves
❖ 4 Tbsp red wine
❖ Freshly ground black
   pepper
❖ 4 lemon wedges, to
   serve

Lay the tuna in a dish. Pound the thyme with the garlic, gradually adding the oil as the garlic is crushed. A heavy pestle and mortar is best for this. Alternatively, process the mixture to a paste in a blender. Stir in the wine and add seasoning, then pour the marinade over the fish. Cover and chill for at least 2 hours. For a full flavor leave the fish overnight.

Preheat the grill to a medium heat, then cook the tuna for 7 to 10 minutes on each side, depending on the thickness of the steak. Brush with the marinade during cooking. Serve with lemon wedges.

Tuna in Fresh Tomato Marinade

This tuna develops a marvelous, rich taste after marinating in the tomato mixture.
All it needs is a simple salad of gourmet mixed leaves in vinaigrette for a perfect meal.

Serves 4
Preparation time: 25 minutes
Marinating time: 2 hours
Cooking time: 14 to 20 minutes

❖ 2 lb fresh tuna steak
❖ 1 onion, finely chopped

❖ 1 garlic clove, crushed
❖ 4 Tbsp olive oil
❖ 1 lb ripe tomatoes,
   chopped
❖ 1 tsp dried oregano
❖ Salt and freshly ground
   black pepper

Place the tuna in a dish. Cook the onion and garlic in the oil over a gentle heat for 10 minutes. Stir in the tomatoes and cook for a further 5 minutes. Press the mixture through a non-metallic sifter. Add the oregano and plenty of seasoning, then leave to cool. Pour the cold marinade over the tuna, cover, and chill for at least 2 hours.

Preheat the grill to medium, then lift the fish from the marinade and cook for 7 to 10 minutes on each side, depending on the thickness of the steak. Brush occasionally with marinade. Heat any remaining marinade to boiling point, then pour it over the grilled tuna before serving.

Bass and Banana Kebobs

This unusual dish makes a great appetizer, or serve as a snack with cocktails.

Serves 4 to 6
Preparation time: 15 minutes
Cooking time: 6 to 10 minutes

❖ 4 Tbsp (½ stick) salted butter, melted; with extra for drizzling

❖ ¼ cup lemon juice
❖ 12 oz sea bass fillets
❖ 3 large bananas, skinned
❖ Strips of lemon rind, to garnish

Combine the melted butter with the lemon juice and set aside. Cut the fish into 1-inch cubes and cut the bananas into chunks. Alternate the fish and the banana on metal skewers, or wooden skewers that have been soaked in water for 30 minutes. Brush with the butter and lemon juice baste.

Preheat the grill to hot. Cook the kebobs, basting and turning frequently, for 6 to 9 minutes until the fish is opaque throughout. Drizzle the extra melted butter over the cooked kebobs, garnish with lemon rind, and serve.

Try substituting fresh peaches for the bananas when they are in season.

Soy-basted Red Snapper

For this dish you can substitute sea bass, pompano, silver mullet, or trout. If preferred, fish steaks or cutlets can be used in place of a whole fish; it is not necessary to slash these, and they will only need to be cooked for 6 to 7 minutes on each side, depending on thickness and type.

Serves 2 to 4
Preparation time: 10 minutes
Cooking time: 12 to 15 minutes

- 1½ lb whole fish, scaled and cleaned
- 1½ Tbsp rice vinegar
- 2 Tbsp sesame oil
- 3 Tbsp soy sauce
- 2 garlic cloves, crushed and finely chopped
- 1-inch piece of fresh ginger, grated
- 1 scallion, white and green part finely sliced
- 1½ Tbsp crushed toasted sesame seeds (see page 23)
- 2 tsp chili powder, or cayenne pepper mixed with paprika
- 2 tsp sugar
- Freshly ground black pepper

With the point of a sharp knife, cut four deep diagonal slashes on each side of the fish. Mix together the remaining ingredients and rub one-third into the fish, taking care to work it deep into the slashes.

Preheat the grill to hot. Cook the fish about 6 inches away from the heat for 6 to 7 minutes a side, basting occasionally with the remainder of the sauce. Transfer the fish to a warm plate and serve.

Shrimp and Bacon Kebobs

These are really simple, tasty kebobs. A great recipe for a novice.

Serves 4
Preparation time: 20 minutes
Cooking time: 10 to 15 minutes

- 4 Tbsp (½ stick) salted butter, melted with extra for drizzling

- ¼ cup lemon juice
- 1 lb fresh shrimp
- 6 to 8 rashers bacon

Combine the melted butter and lemon juice, to use as a basting sauce.

Shell the shrimp, and remove the veins. Remove any rind from the bacon and cut each rasher into halves or thirds, the pieces must be big enough to wrap each shrimp, which is then threaded onto a metal skewer. Brush with the lemon and butter mixture.

Preheat the grill and cook over medium to hot coals until the shrimp are cooked and the bacon is crisp, about 10 to 15 minutes. Turn and baste frequently; baste again just before serving, and serve drizzled with melted butter.

Shrimp and Mussel Packages

*This is a convenient and clean way to cook small shellfish such as shrimp and mussels
which easily fall through the rack. Prepare the packages ahead of time and keep in the refrigerator
until the fire is ready. Serve with good Italian or French bread to mop up the juices.*

Serves 4
Preparation time: 20 minutes
Cooking time: 10 to 12 minutes

For the Garlic butter
✧ 8 Tbsp (1 stick) unsalted
  butter, softened
✧ 1 tsp finely chopped
  parsley

✧ 1 tsp garlic paste
  (see tip)
✧ Salt, optional

✧ 1 lb fresh shrimp in the
  shell
✧ 1½ lb fresh mussels in
  the shell
✧ Lemon wedges, to serve

Beat together the ingredients for the garlic butter,
seasoning with salt to taste, and set aside.

Prepare the shrimp by removing the heads and legs. Wash
the mussels thoroughly under cold running water and
scrub with a brush. Discard any mussels with broken or
cracked shells. Arrange the shrimp in a single layer on an
18-inch rectangle of heavy-duty aluminum foil and dot
with 3 tablespoons of the garlic butter. Fold the package

up loosely, pinching the edges securely to seal. Repeat
with the mussels which will need 2 or 3 foil packages,
depending on their size.

Preheat the grill to medium hot. Cook the packages for
about 10 to 12 minutes, shaking the bundle every couple
of minutes. The mussels are cooked when the shells open
of their own accord; discard any that fail to open. Serve
with lemon wedges.

Tip
Clams and oysters can also be cooked by this method.

Tip
To crush garlic to a paste, peel and press down firmly with
the flat side of the knife to crush slightly. Sprinkle over a
little salt and pulverize the garlic using the tip end of the
knife held flat side down.

Chipotle Shrimp with Smoky Avocado Salsa

Smoky chipotle chiles flavor the marinade for these shrimp.
Use whole or shelled and deveined shrimp according to preference. Serve as an appetizer
or main course with bowls of Smoky Avocado Salsa on the side.

Serves 4 to 6
Preparation time: 30 minutes
Marinating time: 30 minutes
Cooking time: 4 to 6 minutes

For the Kebobs
❖ **2 dried or canned chipotle chiles**
❖ **¼ cup fresh lime juice**
❖ **¼ cup fresh orange juice**
❖ **3 Tbsp olive oil**
❖ **¼ cup chopped fresh cilantro**
❖ **1½ lb medium to large shrimp**

For the Salsa
❖ **2 large, ripe avocados, peeled, stoned, and diced**
❖ **3 Tbsp fresh lime juice**
❖ **¼ cup finely chopped red onion**
❖ **1 canned chipotle chile, finely chopped**
❖ **1 jalapeno or serrano chile, finely chopped**
❖ **1 medium tomato, seeded and chopped**
❖ **1 clove garlic, crushed**
❖ **1 Tbsp olive oil**
❖ **Salt**

If you are using dried chipotles, pour over just enough boiling water to cover them, about ¼ cup. Let them soak for 20 to 30 minutes, then drain and remove the chile stalks. Process soaked or canned chipotles with the lime juice, orange juice, and olive oil in a food processor, then add the cilantro. Put the shrimp in a dish and pour over the marinade. Toss to coat the shrimp completely. Cover and leave to stand for at least 30 minutes, turning once or twice.

To make the salsa, mix the diced avocado with the lime juice. Stir in the remaining ingredients. Taste and adjust seasonings.

While the grill is heating, thread the shrimp onto metal skewers, or wooden skewers soaked in water for 30 minutes. Do not jam them on together or they will cook unevenly. Cook over medium hot coals for about 2 minutes on each side, until the shrimp curl up slightly and are slightly charred on the edges. Serve with the salsa.

Skewered Potatoes with Shrimp

Shrimp marry well with potatoes. Serve with a spicy tomato salsa (see page 72).

Serves 4
Preparation time: 20 minutes
Cooking time: 10 minutes

- 32 small new potatoes, with skins on
- 16 large uncooked shrimp, peeled with tails on
- 2 Tbsp olive oil
- 1 Tbsp salted butter,

melted
- Grated rind and juice of ½ lemon
- Salt and freshly ground black pepper
- 2 Tbsp chopped fresh dill, to garnish

Parboil the potatoes for about 5 minutes, then drain well. Mix the potatoes and shrimp in a bowl with the oil, butter, lemon rind and juice, and seasoning. Toss the shrimp and potatoes gently to coat them completely in the seasonings. When thoroughly coated, thread the ingredients on metal skewers.

Preheat the grill to a medium heat and cook for about 5 minutes on each side, until the potatoes have finished cooking and begun to brown, and the shrimp are cooked through. Garnish with dill and serve at once.

Middle Eastern Seafood Kebobs

Serve these kebobs in pita pockets (see page 30) or on a bed of plain rice with an arugula and orange salad.

Serves 4
Preparation time: 20 minutes
Marinating time: 1 to 2 hours
Cooking time: 4 to 8 minutes

- ¼ cup plain yogurt
- 1 small onion, finely chopped
- 2 garlic cloves
- 2 fresh red chiles, seeded and chopped

- Juice of 1 lime
- Chili powder
- Salt and freshly ground black pepper
- 1½ lb seafood such as shelled, deveined shrimp or crayfish, scallops, lobster meat

Place the yogurt, onion, garlic, chiles, and lime juice in a blender and process to a paste. Add chili powder and season to taste.

Prepare the seafood and place in a ceramic or glass dish. Pour over the marinade and toss to coat. Cover and leave for 1 to 2 hours. When the coals are almost medium hot, thread the seafood onto metal skewers (or wooden skewers soaked in water for 30 minutes), leaving a small space between them to allow even cooking.

Preheat the grill to medium hot and cook the kebobs for about 2 to 4 minutes on each side, or until cooked through.

Lobster-shrimp-scallop Kebobs

*Because most kinds of seafood cook faster than meat,
it is often possible to make garnished kebobs with olives, tomatoes, and
onions, on the skewer along with the fish or shellfish.*

Serves 4
Preparation time: 30 minutes
Cooking time: 8 to 10 minutes

- 8 Tbsp (1 stick) salted butter, melted
- 2 Tbsp lemon juice
- 1 lobster tail
- ½ lb fresh shrimp
- ½ lb shelled fresh scallops
- 24 cherry tomatoes
- 24 large stuffed green olives
- Salt and freshly ground black pepper
- 2 Tbsp finely chopped parsley, to garnish

Combine the melted butter and the lemon juice as a brushing sauce.

Remove the meat from the lobster tail, devein, and cut into chunks. Shell and devein the shrimp. Thread the lobster, shrimp, scallops, tomatoes, and olives on the skewers and sprinkle with salt and pepper.

Preheat the grill to hot, then grill the skewers until the seafood is cooked through and opaque, about 8 to 10 minutes. Turn and baste frequently. Garnish with the parsley and serve.

Twice-cooked Scallop Kebobs

*Twice-cooked because the rice vinegar begins to "cook" the scallops in the same
way that lime juice "cooks" fish when making Mexican seviche (raw fish marinated in citrus juice),
so the scallops need only brief cooking on the grill if they are not to become overcooked.*

Serves 2 to 4
Preparation time: 15 minutes
Marinating time: 30 minutes
Cooking time: 3 to 4 minutes

❖ 12 large scallops
❖ 1 garlic clove, crushed
   and finely chopped
❖ 1 Tbsp finely chopped
   scallion, green part only

❖ 2 Tbsp soy sauce
❖ 2 tsp rice vinegar
❖ 1 Tbsp sesame oil
❖ ½-inch piece of fresh
   ginger, grated
❖ 2 tsp crushed toasted
   sesame seeds (see
   page 23)
❖ pinch of chili powder

Cut each scallop in half horizontally. Thread the scallops onto skewers and lay them in a shallow dish.

Mix together the remaining ingredients and pour over the scallops. Turn the skewers over, cover, and leave for 30 minutes, turning occasionally.

Preheat the grill to medium hot. Lift the skewers from the marinade and cook for 3 to 4 minutes, turning occasionally and brushing with the marinade.

Herb-crumbed Lobster Tail

*This elegant dish was inspired by the lobster served at the Runaway Hill
Club in the Bahamas.*

Serves 4
Preparation time: 20 minutes
Cooking time: 15 to 20 minutes

❖ 4 lobster tails (about
   1½ lb in total), thawed
   if frozen, removed from
   shells intact and
   deveined
❖ 4 tsp fresh lime or
   lemon juice
❖ 4 garlic cloves, crushed
❖ 6 Tbsp (¾ stick) unsalted
   butter
❖ 1 cup dry bread crumbs

❖ 2 tsp salt
❖ 1 tsp freshly ground
   black pepper
❖ ½ tsp dried thyme
❖ ½ tsp dried marjoram
❖ ½ tsp dried oregano
❖ ½ tsp dried basil
❖ ½ tsp dried rosemary
❖ ½ tsp dried sage
❖ ½ tsp garlic powder
❖ ¼ tsp hot pepper sauce
❖ 2 Tbsp freshly grated
   Parmesan cheese
❖ Corn oil

Rinse the lobster shells and dry with paper towels, then sprinkle them with lime or lemon juice. In a small saucepan, cook the garlic in the butter over moderate heat for about 1 minute. Remove the pan from the heat.

In a shallow bowl, stir together the bread crumbs, salt, pepper, thyme, marjoram, oregano, basil, rosemary, sage, garlic powder, hot pepper sauce, and Parmesan cheese. Roll the pieces of lobster meat in the garlic butter, dredge them in the bread crumb mixture, and return them to the shells.

Preheat the grill to medium hot and brush the rack with oil. Grill the tails, shell sides down, on a rack set 4 to 6 inches over the coals, for 10 minutes, turning them occasionally from side to side. Cover the barbecue if possible, and grill tails for 5 to 10 minutes more or until they are just cooked through.

Chapter

6

Succulent, Smoky Vegetables

Why not serve cooked vegetables in place of salads? Most vegetables grill successfully, from eggplant to bell peppers, onions to sweet potatoes. Many develop a delicious, crispy skin with a smoky aroma and, because they cook in their own juices, their natural flavor is intensified. Spray or brush the vegetables with a little oil to help keep them moist and tender, and oil the rack to prevent sticking. Some of the vegetable recipes here suggest the use of a foil package. This method prevents small pieces falling through the rack and produces an intensely flavored result; try the Mushroom Pockets or the Caramelized Onions with Rosemary just once and you'll be hooked.

Vegetable Burgers with Salsa

Serve these burgers in fresh buns with a little salad garnish and a dollop of sour cream.

Serves 8
Preparation time: 30 minutes
Chilling time: 2 hours
Cooking time: 15 minutes

For the Burgers
- Two 15-oz cans garbanzo beans, drained
- 1 cup canned, or fresh cooked corn, drained
- 1 bunch scallions, roughly chopped
- 2 large garlic cloves, finely chopped
- 2 Tbsp salted butter, melted
- 2 Tbsp finely chopped parsley
- 1 Tbsp wine vinegar
- 2 Tbsp chopped fresh mint
- 2 cups soft bread crumbs
- About 8 Tbsp sesame seeds
- Corn oil

For the Salsa
- 3 ripe tomatoes, diced
- 4 scallions, thinly sliced
- 1 large garlic clove, finely chopped
- 1 hot chile pepper, seeded, and finely chopped
- ¼ cup chopped fresh cilantro

Put all the ingredients for the burgers, except the last three, into a food processor and blend until smooth. Stir in the bread crumbs. Divide the mixture into eight and shape each one into a burger. Coat with sesame seeds, pressing them into the surface. Cover and refrigerate for at least 2 hours.

Meanwhile, make the salsa. Mix together the tomatoes, scallions, garlic, chile pepper, and cilantro. Cover and leave to stand until needed.

Preheat the grill to medium hot. Brush the burgers lightly with oil and cook for about 15 minutes, turning carefully once or twice. Serve immediately in buns accompanied by the salsa.

RIGHT: VEGETABLE BURGERS WITH SALSA

Grilled Corn

There are two ways to grill corn: with the husk and without. Grilling with the husks gives a tender, juicier ear, but grilling without results in a flavor and texture all its own.

Serves 4
Preparation time: 5 to 10 minutes
Soaking time: 30 minutes
Cooking time: 3 to 5 minutes, or 20 minutes

- 4 ears of corn
- Salt and freshly ground black pepper, to serve
- Salted butter, to serve

Corn in the husk First remove the silk (the threads between the husk and the corn). This means peeling back the husk, so do it as carefully as possible. You may need to secure the husk with florists' wire (but *not* the plastic-coated kind!) when you replace it.

Soak the corn in ice-water for at least 30 minutes, then roast it over a medium, direct fire for about 20 minutes, turning frequently. To check if the corn is cooked, prick a kernel with a knife; if it spurts clear juice, it is done.

Parched corn The corn is cooked without the husk. Bring a large pan of water to the boil, and plunge the ears of corn into it for no more than a couple of minutes. Then finish the corn on a medium or medium-hot grill for another 3 to 5 minutes, depending on the heat, turning frequently.

Plain grilled corn Cook the ears of corn over a low heat for 10 to 20 minutes. Once again, turn frequently. Serve with salt only.

Ember-cooked Vegetables with Flavored Butters

*These slow-cooked vegetables are delicious served with any one of
the flavored butters suggested on page 75. The vegetables cook best with the air vent shut right down and the top
closed so that the embers smolder at the lowest temperature possible. If you do not have a lid,
try using a double layer of heavy-duty aluminum foil.*

Potatoes cooked in the embers

Potatoes are the obvious choice for ember cooking. If you are not planning to use foil, oil the skin to reduce charring. A medium-size potato should take between ¾ to 1 hour to cook fully. Turn often, using tongs.
The potatoes will require far less attention if you wrap them in foil before putting them in the embers but, somehow, it isn't the same. They will take 5 to 10 minutes longer to cook, too.

Squash cooked in the embers

A less obvious choice, but arguably even more effective, is cooking squash or pumpkin in the embers. Oil the outside, slash the skin deeply (to prevent it bursting open), and turn frequently during a cooking time of 45 to 60 minutes.

Onions cooked in the embers

These are a real surprise. Use large, sweet onions. Cut off the ends (which would otherwise burn), but do not peel them: just put them snugly into the embers and leave them for about 45 minutes, turning fairly frequently. The outer skin will be blackened and inedible and should be thrown away, but the onion inside is delicious.

Other vegetables in embers

You can cook almost any vegetable in this way, but you should wrap it in heavy-duty aluminum foil first. With more delicate vegetables, such as zucchini, use a double layer of foil to reduce the risk of charring. Corn will cook in the embers in about 20 minutes; zucchinis, individually wrapped, in about 15 to 20 minutes; and mushrooms, with butter, in about 10 to 15 minutes, depending on the size of the parcel.

Halved vegetables

Cutting potatoes and squashes in half, lengthways, makes it easier to cook them evenly all the way through. Protecting the cut side with aluminum foil not only promotes moistness and prevents charring, it also slows down the rate of heat transfer, as the foil reflects a good deal of the heat, and makes it easier to cook evenly, even if it takes longer. For either potatoes or pumpkin, the cooking time is about 60 minutes. Begin with the foil side faced down but after 35 to 40 minutes, turn the vegetables and cook the other side for the remaining time. The foil can be removed when you turn the vegetables over.

Flavored Butters

These butters are best made in advance to allow the flavors to develop.
They add a touch of luxurious piquancy to the ember-cooked vegetables.

Herbed butter

- 4 Tbsp (½ stick) unsalted butter
- 2 tsp lemon juice
- Salt and freshly ground black pepper
- 1 Tbsp chopped fresh tarragon, dill, cilantro, oregano, or parsley

Blend all ingredients together, chill, and use on grilled vegetables. The lemon flavor goes particularly well with zucchini.

Green butter

- 1½ cups spinach leaves, washed
- 1 bunch watercress, stalks removed
- 1 garlic clove
- Fresh tarragon, to taste
- A few sprigs of parsley
- Fresh chives, to taste
- ½ sweet dill pickle
- 1 tsp capers
- 3 anchovy fillets
- 2 Tbsp oil
- 1 egg yolk
- 1 hard-cooked egg
- 8 Tbsp (1 stick) unsalted butter, softened

It is easiest to make this excellent butter in a blender, otherwise all ingredients have to be chopped by hand.

Drop the spinach leaves, watercress, garlic, and herbs into the processor and purée. Add the dill pickle, capers, and anchovy fillets with the oil, egg yolk, and hard-cooked egg. Lastly blend in the softened butter. This is especially good with barbecued potatoes and pumpkin.

Garlic butter

- 4 Tbsp (½ stick) unsalted butter, softened
- 1 to 2 garlic cloves, crushed
- 2 tsp chopped parsley

Beat the butter and add the well-crushed garlic and parsley. Blend well. Chill well and serve with ember-cooked onions.

Anchovy butter

- 6 anchovy fillets
- 2 Tbsp milk
- 6 Tbsp (¾ stick) unsalted butter
- Freshly ground black pepper
- Hot pepper sauce, to taste

Soak the anchovy fillets briefly in milk. Mash in a bowl with a wooden spoon until creamy. Beat all ingredients together, adding hot pepper sauce to taste. Chill and serve with potatoes.

Mustard butter

- 4 Tbsp (½ stick) unsalted butter
- 1 Tbsp whole-grain mustard
- Salt and freshly ground black pepper

Beat all the ingredients together and chill. Serve with butternut squash.

Vegetable Kebobs with Honey-mustard Glaze

*Cooking both meat and vegetables on the same skewer is possible, but
risky: all too often, the meat will still be half-raw when the vegetables are either burning or falling
apart. A much better idea is to grill vegetable kebobs separately. Only experience will teach you exactly
what sizes to cut the various vegetables that can be cooked together on a skewer, but you
might care to try the following recipe to compare a selection of vegetables.*

Serves 4

Preparation time: 20 minutes

Marinating time: 1 to 2 hours

- ❖ **12 oz young pumpkin or squash, seeded**
- ❖ **1 small eggplant**
- ❖ **2 bell peppers red, green, or yellow, seeded**
- ❖ **1 medium red onion**
- ❖ **8 cherry tomatoes**

- ❖ **½ cup olive oil**
- ❖ **5 tsp cider or wine vinegar**
- ❖ **1 Tbsp chopped fresh thyme**
- ❖ **2 Tbsp chopped parsley**
- ❖ **2 Tbsp honey**
- ❖ **2 Tbsp whole-grain mustard**
- ❖ **Fresh thyme, to garnish**

Cut the pumpkin or squash and the eggplant into 1-inch cubes. Cut the bell peppers into 1-inch squares. Peel the onion and cut into quarters.

Combine the oil, cider or vinegar, thyme, and parsley, and use to marinade all the vegetables: a plastic self-seal bag is the easiest container to use. Shake the bag occasionally to

ensure even coating, but be careful to avoid breaking up the onions. Leave for 1 to 2 hours.

Preheat the grill to medium, then thread the vegetables onto a skewer, alternating the types. Add the honey and mustard to the remaining marinade. Cook, turning frequently and basting with marinade, for 10 to 15 minutes. By this time, the tomatoes will be very soft indeed. Garnish with the thyme, and serve.

Tip

If you want to add carrots, parboil them for about 3 to 4 minutes or they may be excessively crunchy. Mushrooms should be steamed for a couple of minutes, or there is a real danger that they will split and fall off the skewer.

Barbecued Eggplant with Spicy Pepper Butter

An unusual appetizer to keep the folks happy while the meat is cooking on the grill. Serve with soft rolls or pita bread.

Serves 4

Preparation time: 10 minutes

Plus chilling time: 1 hour

Cooking time: 40 minutes

For the Spicy Pepper Butter
* 8 Tbsp (1 stick) salted butter
* 1 tsp finely chopped onion
* 1 garlic clove, crushed

* ½ tsp paprika
* ½ tsp green peppercorns, crushed
* 1 Tbsp chopped fresh cilantro
* Salt and freshly ground black pepper
* 2 eggplants
* Cilantro leaves, to garnish

To make the spicy butter, beat the butter in a bowl with a wooden spoon until soft, then add all the remaining seasonings, with salt and pepper to taste. Shape the butter into a roll, then cover in plastic wrap and chill for 1 hour.

Preheat the grill until the coals are moderately hot. Cook the eggplants for about 20 minutes until the skins are

blistered and wrinkled, and the flesh is tender. Turn them over several times during cooking. Do not cook them too quickly or the skins will burst.

Carefully remove the eggplants from the grill, then cut them in half lengthways. Score the soft flesh into diamonds, then top with a generous knob of the spicy butter. Garnish with cilantro leaves, and serve.

Roasted Eggplant Dip

This dip is good served warm, or it may be cooled and chilled lightly before serving. It makes a good appetizer, with pita bread, or it may be mounded on split baked potatoes. It also tastes good with grilled lamb chops or steaks.

Serves 4

Preparation time: 5 minutes

Cooking time: 15 to 20 minutes

Finishing time: 15 minutes

* 2 large eggplants
* 2 garlic cloves, crushed
* 2 Tbsp tahini (sesame paste)

* ½ cup olive oil
* 2 Tbsp lemon juice
* Generous pinch ground nutmeg
* Salt and freshly ground black pepper

Roast the eggplants over medium heat on a covered grill if possible, until they are soft through and well browned outside, about 15 to 20 minutes, turning two or three times.

Halve the eggplants and scrape all the soft flesh off the skin into a bowl. Mash the eggplant flesh thoroughly with the garlic until it is smooth, or use a food processor. Beat in the tahini, then gradually beat in the olive oil, drop by drop at first. As the oil is incorporated it can be added a little faster. Beat well until smooth and creamy. Stir in the lemon juice, a little nutmeg, and seasoning.

Grilled Eggplant with Tomato

Serve with crusty bread as an appetizer or with grilled meat.

Serves 4
Preparation time: 35 minutes
Cooking time: 10 to 15 minutes

❖ 2 large eggplants
❖ Salt
❖ 1 onion, finely chopped
❖ 1 garlic clove, crushed

❖ 4 to 6 Tbsp olive oil
❖ 8 tomatoes, peeled and sliced
❖ Salt and freshly ground black pepper

Cut the eggplants in half lengthways, leaving their stalks on. Sprinkle the cut sides generously with salt, place eggplants in a dish, and leave for 30 minutes. Rinse off the salt and dry the eggplants on paper towels.

Meanwhile, cook the onion and garlic in 2 tablespoons of the olive oil for about 10 minutes, until the onion is thoroughly softened and just beginning to brown. Add the tomato slices and season generously with salt and pepper. Set aside.

Brush the eggplants all over with olive oil, then cook them skin sides down over medium heat for 5 minutes, until well browned. Brush with more oil and turn the cut sides down, then cook for a further 5 minutes or so, until tender and browned.

Place the cooked eggplants on a flat dish and slice them from the stalk, outwards to make fan shapes. Quickly heat the tomato mixture, then spoon it between the eggplant slices. Serve immediately.

Onions with Mustard, Lemon, and Herbs

Allow your guests to open their own package—they will want to enjoy every scrap of onion, some of which will be caramelized and stuck to the foil.

Serves 8
Preparation time: 10 minutes
Cooking time: 20 minutes

❖ 4 large onions, peeled
❖ 8 Tbsp (1 stick) butter
❖ 4 Tbsp whole-grain mustard

❖ 2 Tbsp fresh lemon juice
❖ 1 Tbsp sugar
❖ 4 Tbsp finely chopped fresh herbs, such as parsley, thyme, or oregano
❖ Salt and freshly ground black pepper

Cut eight large rectangles of heavy-duty aluminum foil. Thickly slice the onions into rings and arrange on the foil. Melt the butter in a small pan and stir in the remaining ingredients. Spoon the mixture over the onions. Fold the foil over the onions, sealing the edges to make packages.

Arrange on the preheated grill and cook over medium coals for about 20 minutes, turning frequently, or until the onions are very soft and caramelized.

Caramelized Onions with Rosemary

Baby onions and fresh rosemary sprigs are wrapped in foil and grilled. Serve the packages intact so that your guests can marvel at the aroma as they tear open the foil.

Serves 4

Preparation time: 10 minutes

Cooking time: 15 minutes

❖ About 32 baby onions or shallots, peeled, and left whole

❖ 8 sprigs rosemary

❖ 3 Tbsp olive oil

❖ 1 Tbsp balsamic vinegar

❖ 1 tsp sugar

❖ Freshly ground black pepper

Cut four large squares of heavy-duty aluminum foil and put about 8 onions and 2 rosemary sprigs on each. Gather the foil up slightly to make an open pouch. Whisk together the remaining ingredients and drizzle over the onions and rosemary. Close the pouches, sealing them well.

Preheat the grill to medium-hot. Arrange the foil packages on the rack and cook for about 15 minutes, turning occasionally, until the onions are soft and slightly caramelized.

Kebobs of Shiitake Mushrooms, Tofu, and Onion

*This makes a good appetizer or vegetarian main course served on rice with peas and orange
bell pepper. It's delicious served at room temperature, too, so toss some on the fire when you are having
a cook-out, and enjoy them at room temperature as an appetizer the next day.*

Serves 4

Preparation time: 40 to 45
minutes

Marinating time: $1/2$ to 12 hours

Cooking time: 5 to 10 minutes

* 6 to 8 fresh shiitake
  mushrooms, quartered
* 12 oz tofu, cut into bite-
  size chunks
* 3 to 4 onions, cut into
  bite-size chunks
* 5 garlic cloves, chopped
* 3 to 5 Tbsp soy sauce

* 1 Tbsp lime or lemon
  juice
* Several shakes of Tabasco
  sauce
* 2 Tbsp sesame oil
* $1/2$ tsp ground cumin
* $1/4$ tsp ground coriander
* 1 Tbsp finely shredded or
  chopped fresh ginger
* Several pinches of
  Chinese five-spice
  powder
* 3 Tbsp corn oil

Place the shiitakes, tofu, and onions in a shallow dish and
sprinkle with the remaining ingredients, turning
everything so that it is all evenly coated. Cover and leave
to marinate at room temperature for at least 30 minutes
or preferably overnight in the refrigerator, turning several
times.

Preheat the grill to medium. Thread the shiitake, tofu, and
onion onto metal skewers, then cook over the grill for 5 to
10 minutes. Serve hot or at room temperature.

Garlic Mushrooms with Cilantro

This one is for real garlic lovers! The garlic is cooked whole until it is really soft, then squeezed over the grilled mushrooms.

Serves 4
Preparation time: 2 minutes
Cooking time: 40 minutes

⬥ 4 small garlic bulbs
⬥ Olive oil
⬥ 4 large, flat mushrooms

⬥ **Salt and freshly ground black pepper**
⬥ **4 Tbsp chopped fresh cilantro**
⬥ **4 lemon wedges, to serve**

Remove the garlic stems by slicing the top off the garlic bulbs. Brush liberally with olive oil and wrap all 4 bulbs together loosely in heavy-duty aluminum foil. Place on the grill and cook over medium-hot coals for about 30 minutes, turning frequently, or until the garlic is really soft.

Allow to cool slightly while you cook the mushrooms.

Lightly brush the mushrooms with oil, and season with salt and pepper. Cook on the grill over high heat for about 10 minutes, turning occasionally, or until golden brown and just cooked.

Sprinkle the mushrooms with the chopped cilantro. Serve each person with a mushroom, a garlic bulb, and a lemon wedge. Use fingers to squeeze the garlic "purée" out of the cloves and on to the mushroom. Squeeze the lemon juice over and enjoy!

Mushroom Pockets

Cooking mushrooms in foil packages traps all the juices, making the cooked vegetable moist and full of flavor. Try cooking some of the more exotic mushrooms such as oyster or shiitake by this method.

Serves 4
Preparation time: 15 minutes
Cooking time: 15 minutes

⬥ **1 lb mushrooms**
⬥ **8 Tbsp (1 stick) salted butter**
⬥ **Salt and freshly ground black pepper**

Wash and trim the mushrooms, and if they are really big, slice them. Divide the prepared mushrooms into 4 portions and place each on a large piece of heavy-duty

aluminum foil. Dot the mushrooms in each parcel with 2 tablespoons of butter, season to taste, and wrap the packages securely. Preheat the grill to hot and cook for about 15 minutes, turning occasionally. The mushrooms are cooked when they are tender, but a little overcooking (even 5 to 10 minutes) will do no harm.

Garlic lovers should slice a single clove of garlic into 4 pieces, lengthways, and add a slice to each parcel. For real luxury, substitute the heaviest cream you can find for the butter, using 4 tablespoons in each package.

Barbecued Portobellos

Be sure to marinate the portobellos, for that extra dimension.
Olive oil, lemon juice or balsamic or sherry vinegar, and lots of garlic or shallots,
make the best marinade, boosted with fresh thyme, tarragon, or parsley.

Serves 4

Preparation time: 10 minutes

Marinating time: 15 to 30
   minutes

Cooking time: 10 minutes

❖ 2 large portobellos as a
   side dish, 4 as a main
   course

❖ 3 to 5 garlic cloves,
   chopped
❖ 2 to 3 Tbsp olive oil
❖ Juice of ½ lemon or 1
   Tbsp sherry or balsamic
   vinegar
❖ Salt, freshly ground black
   pepper, parsley, and
   thyme

Sprinkle the mushrooms with the garlic, olive oil, lemon juice or vinegar, and seasonings. Leave for 15 to 30 minutes.

Place on a preheated medium grill, preferably one with a cover, ensuring the food is surrounded by hot, smoky heat. Cook for about 10 minutes, turning once or twice, letting the mushrooms cook until lightly browned but juicy inside. Serve immediately, whole or sliced.

Potatoes with Blue Cheese and Walnuts

Cook these small, whole potatoes on skewers or in a wire mesh grill basket.

Serves 6

Preparation time: 20 minutes +
   cooling time

Cooking time: 15 minutes

❖ About 1½ lb small
   potatoes
❖ ¼ cup walnut oil
❖ ¼ cup sunflower oil

❖ ¼ cup Dijon or whole-
   grain mustard
❖ 2 Tbsp lemon juice
❖ 1 cup crumbled blue
   cheese
❖ ½ cup finely chopped
   walnuts

Cook the potatoes, in their skins, in boiling water for about 15 minutes or until just tender. Drain and tip into a large bowl. Whisk together the oils, mustard, and lemon juice. Pour over the hot potatoes and stir gently until well coated. Cover and allow to cool, stirring gently from time to time. Blend together the blue cheese and walnuts. Cover until needed.

Preheat the grill to medium hot and cook the potatoes on skewers or in a wire basket for about 15 minutes, turning occasionally, or until crisp and golden brown. To serve, split the potatoes and top each one with a small spoonful of the cheese mixture.

Spiced Potatoes with Sour Cream Dressing

*These thick discs of potato are topped with a dollop of
sour cream and a sprinkling of chives. Serve them as an appetizer or with
the main course. Use freshly grated nutmeg if you can.*

Serves 8 to 10
Preparation time: 10 minutes
Cooking time: 15 minutes

- ❖ **8 Tbsp (1 stick) salted butter**
- ❖ **1 tsp paprika**
- ❖ **½ tsp salt**
- ❖ **½ tsp freshly ground black pepper**
- ❖ **¼ freshly grated nutmeg**
- ❖ **4 large potatoes, scrubbed**
- ❖ **1 cup sour cream, to serve**
- ❖ **4 Tbsp chopped fresh chives, to serve**

Melt the butter and stir in the paprika, salt, pepper, and nutmeg. Cut the potatoes into thick slices and brush each side with the butter mixture.

Preheat the grill to medium. Arrange the potatoes on the rack and cook for about 15 minutes, turning occasionally, until crisp on the outside and tender in the middle. Top with a dollop of sour cream and chives. Serve.

Sweet Potato with Coconut Curry Glaze

This recipe is just as delicious if the partially cooked sweet potato and the coconut sauce are wrapped in foil and grilled.

Serves 8

Preparation time: 20 minutes

Marinating time: 1 to 2 hours

Cooking time: 10 to 15 minutes

❖ **About 2 lb sweet potatoes, peeled and cut into 1-inch cubes**
❖ **1 Tbsp lime juice**
❖ **1 cup coconut cream**

❖ **4 scallions, finely chopped**
❖ **1 Tbsp curry powder**
❖ **1 tsp sugar**
❖ **Salt and freshly ground black pepper**
❖ **Lime wedges, to serve**
❖ **Parsley, to garnish**

Bring the sweet potatoes to a boil in lightly salted water and cook for about 5 minutes, or until just cooked but still firm. Drain well. Mix together the remaining ingredients, add the potatoes, and stir until well coated. Cover and allow to stand for 1 to 2 hours.

Thread on to skewers and arrange on the preheated grill. Cook over medium-hot coals for 10 to 15 minutes, turning occasionally, until golden brown. Serve with lime wedges, garnished with parsley, and serve immediately with any remaining coconut sauce spooned over.

Tip

Coconut cream is available in some markets, specialty food stores, and Asian markets. It can come in liquid or powder form, or in a solid block. Reconstitute following manufacturer's instructions.

Grilled Zucchini Platter with Orange and Ginger Marinade

*A surprising variety of vegetables can be cooked in a wire mesh grill basket,
especially delicate vegetables which are prone to falling apart just when they are ready to
be served. The vegetables can be cooked simply in an oiled basket basted with olive oil or
butter during cooking; alternatively, they may be cooked in a marinade.*

Serves 4 to 6
Preparation time: 15 minutes
Marinating time: 1 hour
Cooking time: 6 to 10 minutes

- ❖ 4 small green zucchini
- ❖ 4 small yellow zucchini
- ❖ 1 cup orange juice
- ❖ 4 Tbsp lemon juice
- ❖ 1 Tbsp grated fresh
  ginger
- ❖ 4 Tbsp light soy sauce
- ❖ 1 Tbsp white wine
  vinegar
- ❖ 1 large garlic clove,
  crushed
- ❖ ½ tsp freshly ground
  mixed pepper, with extra
  to decorate
- ❖ Corn oil

If your zucchini are ¾-inch thick or less, then they may be cooked whole; cut fatter zucchini in half lengthways. Pierce the skin of the zucchini all over with a toothpick or needle to allow the marinade to penetrate the skin. Lay the zucchini in a single layer in a dish. Combine all the remaining ingredients, except the oil, and pour over the zucchini. Cover and marinate for 1 hour.

Preheat the grill to a medium heat. Oil the grill basket thoroughly (a vegetable oil spray is useful for this task). Carefully lay the zucchini in the basket and cook, turning frequently and basting with the marinade while cooking. The zucchini should cook in 6 to 10 minutes, depending on their thickness. The zucchini may need to be cooked in 2 batches if your grill basket is too small to fit the zucchini comfortably in one layer.

Serve decorated with mixed ground pepper.

Zucchini with Parmesan and Herbs

*Cook the zucchini in a wire mesh grill basket, for easy turning.
Open the basket before adding the cheese and herbs. For the best
flavor, use freshly grated Parmesan.*

Serves 4
Preparation time: 2 minutes
Cooking time: 12 minutes

* **8 small-to-medium
  zucchinis, halved
  lengthways**
* **Olive oil**

* **Salt and freshly ground
  black pepper**
* **4 Tbsp finely grated
  Parmesan cheese**
* **4 Tbsp finely chopped
  mixed herbs**

Lightly brush both sides of the zucchini with oil. Season lightly with salt and pepper.

Arrange the zucchini in a basket on the preheated grill and cook over medium-hot coals for about 10 minutes, turning occasionally, or until golden and just cooked. Sprinkle with the Parmesan and herbs, and cook, without turning, for a few minutes longer.

Sweet Squash Wedges

Butter and brown sugar give a lovely crisp finish to the buttery squash.

Serves 4
Preparation time: 10 minutes
Cooking time: 5 to 10 minutes

* **1 small acorn squash,
  quartered and seeded**
* **2 Tbsp (¼ stick) salted
  butter, melted**

* **2 Tbsp chopped fresh
  cilantro**
* **2 tsp granulated brown
  sugar**
* **Extra butter, to serve**

Put the squash quarters into a saucepan and bring to a boil in lightly salted water. Simmer gently for about 5 minutes, or until just cooked but still firm. Drain well.

Brush the squash flesh with the melted butter and sprinkle with the cilantro and sugar.

Preheat the grill to hot. Arrange the squash on the rack and cook for 5 to 10 minutes, or until golden brown. Serve, flesh side up, with a generous knob of butter on top of each wedge.

Chapter

7

Hot, Flambéed Desserts

When we think of grilled food, we immediately think of steaks and hamburgers, but sweet foods, particularly fruits, are wonderful straight from the grill. They are quick to cook, too; all they generally require is heating through long enough to soften and caramelize their natural sugars. It is certainly simpler to make Apples with Fruit and Nuts than to make apple pie.

For a hot and cold sensation, serve these succulent grilled desserts with a scoop of vanilla ice cream, or with lashings of fresh cream. For a healthier alternative, serve with a good organic, fat-free plain yogurt.

Grilled Pineapple with Coconut Cream

No fresh pineapple? Use drained canned rings instead.

Serves 6
Preparation time: 15 minutes
Cooking time: 4 minutes

❖ **1 cup heavy cream**
❖ **1 Tbsp coconut liqueur**
❖ **½ cup coconut cream**
  (see note page 84)

❖ **4 Tbsp (½ stick) unsalted butter**
❖ **1 tsp allspice**
❖ **1 small pineapple, skinned, cored, and cut into six slices**

Whip the cream and liqueur to make stiff peaks. Fold in the coconut cream, cover, and chill until required.

Melt the butter and stir in the mixed spice. Brush the mixture all over the pineapple slices.

Preheat the grill to medium-high. Arrange the pineapple on the rack and cook for about 2 minutes on each side, or until slightly charred and heated through. Serve immediately with the coconut cream.

Sticky Bananas

A favorite with kids and anyone who has a sweet tooth.
The marshmallows melt over the banana to make a deliciously gooey
dessert. Serve alone or with a spoonful of plain yogurt or sour cream.

Serves 4
Preparation time: 5 minutes
Cooking time: 10 to 12 minutes

❖ **4 bananas**
❖ **1 cup mini marshmallows**

❖ **4 tsp fresh lemon juice**
❖ **¼ cup toasted coconut
   shavings**

Using a sharp knife, split the unpeeled bananas along their length, without cutting through the bottom skin. Ease them open to make a cavity in each. Place each banana on a large piece of heavy-duty aluminum foil. Sprinkle the marshmallows in the cavities, pushing them in when necessary. Sprinkle the lemon juice over, then top with the coconut. Gather up the foil over the bananas, securing the seams, to make packages.

Preheat the grill to medium. Arrange the parcels on the rack, seam sides up, and cook for 10 to 12 minutes until soft. Serve immediately, in the foil.

Spiced Fruit Salad

The addition of a fruit tea bag gives a delightful flavor to these parcels of fruit.
They are great for serving on a cool evening. Serve with heavy whipping cream or thick plain yogurt.

Serves 6
Preparation time: 5 minutes
Marinating time: 2 hours
Cooking time: 15 to 20 minutes

❖ **About 1 lb ready-to-eat
   dried fruit, such as
   apricots, pears, figs,
   dates, prunes, apples**

❖ **Three 2-inch cinnamon
   sticks**
❖ **1 cup apple juice**
❖ **Pinch of ground cloves**
❖ **4 Tbsp superfine sugar**
❖ **6 fruit tea bags, such as
   blackcurrant**

Cut 6 large squares of thick foil, gathering up the edges slightly to form a "bowl." Spoon the fruit evenly on to the foil, making sure that each piece has a tea bag and half a cinnamon stick. Gather up the foil to make pouch-style parcels.

Arrange on the grill and cook over medium-low heat for 15 to 20 minutes. Serve in the foil.

Put the fruit into a bowl and stir in the remaining ingredients. Cover and allow to stand for about 2 hours, stirring occasionally.

Cinnamon Bagel Sticks with Apricot Coulis

A coulis is a thick purée or sauce. The bagels can be replaced with sourdough or chunks of any firm bread.
Some of the fruit goes on the sticks, and the rest is made into a refreshing sauce.

Serves 4
Preparation time: 15 minutes
Cooking time: 10 minutes

- 4 oz (½ stick) unsalted butter, softened
- 1 Tbsp granulated brown sugar
- ½ tsp ground cinnamon
- 2 bagels
- Two 15-oz cans apricot halves in juice
- Confectioners' sugar

Blend together the butter, brown sugar, and cinnamon to make a smooth paste. Using a sharp knife, split the bagels in half horizontally. Spread the cut sides with the butter mixture. Cut each half into about 6 pieces. Drain the apricots, reserving the juice. Alternate the bagel pieces and apricot halves on metal skewers, or wooden skewers soaked in water for 30 minutes.

Put the remaining apricots into a blender and process until smooth. With the blender still running, add enough reserved fruit juice to make a thick but still pourable sauce. Sweeten with confectioners' sugar to taste.

Preheat the grill to medium and put the bagel sticks on the rack. Cook for about 10 minutes, turning them once or twice. Serve immediately with the sauce.

Black Bananas with Maple Pecan Syrup

Banana skins form a natural wrapper for cooking on the barbecue.
The Maple Pecan Syrup adds a special touch. For a really decadent dessert, serve with heavy whipping cream.

Serves 4
Preparation time: 5 minutes
Cooking time: 15 minutes

❖ ¼ cup finely chopped
   pecan nuts
❖ ½ tsp allspice
❖ 4 large bananas

❖ ½ cup maple syrup

Mix together the maple syrup, pecan nuts, and mixed spice.

Put the unpeeled bananas on the preheated grill and cook over medium coals for about 15 minutes, turning occasionally until black all over.

Lift the bananas on to a plate. Make a slit along each one, pulling the skin back gently. Drizzle with the maple sauce and serve immediately.

Summer Fruit Packages

Cooking fruit in packages preserves the delicate flesh and seals in all the
flavor. Serve with heavy whipping cream or ice cream for a 'hot n cold' dessert.

Serves 4
Preparation time: 15 minutes
Cooking time: 10 minutes

❖ ½ pt (8 oz) strawberries,
   hulled
❖ ½ pt (8 oz) cherries,
   pitted
❖ 2 peaches

❖ 2 kiwi fruit, peeled and
   sliced
❖ 4 Tbsp (½ stick) unsalted
   butter
❖ 2 Tbsp brown sugar
❖ Grated rind and juice of
   1 orange
❖ 4 sprigs mint

Place the strawberries in a bowl with the cherries. Pour freshly boiling water over the peaches, leave them to

stand for 1 minute, run under cold water, and peel them. Cut the peaches in half, discard their pits, and slice the fruit. Add to the strawberry mixture with the kiwi fruit and mix gently.

Cut 4 large squares of heavy-duty aluminum foil and divide the fruit among them. Heat the butter, sugar, orange rind, and juice until the sugar has melted. Spoon this mixture over the fruit and top each portion with a sprig of mint. Fold the foil around the fruit to seal it in. Preheat the grill to medium, put the fruit packages on the rack, and cook for about 10 minutes.

Bananas in Honey and Lemon Sauce

*Slice the bananas thickly, or leave them whole if you wish;
either way they are delicious. Serve them with vanilla ice cream
or a spoonful of thick plain yogurt.*

Serves 8
Preparation time: 10 minutes
**Cooking time: 10 to 12
    minutes**

❖ **½ cup clear honey**

❖ **2 Tbsp (¼ stick) unsalted
    butter**
❖ **¼ cup lemon juice**
❖ **Finely grated rind of 1
    lemon**
❖ **8 bananas**

In a small pan, gently heat the honey and butter until melted. Stir in the lemon juice and rind.

Cut 8 large rectangles of heavy-duty aluminum foil. Peel and thickly slice the bananas onto the foil. Drizzle the honey mixture over the top. Gather up the foil to make 8 pouch-style packages.

Arrange the packages on the preheated grill, seam sides up. Cook over medium heat for 10 to 12 minutes until soft. Serve immediately, in the foil.

Glazed Pears

This adaptation of pears in red wine is a sophisticated way to end an evening party.

Serves 4
Preparation time: 20 minutes
Cooking time: 5 to 8 minutes

❖ **6 large, firm ripe pears,
    peeled, cored, and
    halved**
❖ **Grated rind and juice of
    ½ lemon**
❖ **4 Tbsp maple syrup**
❖ **1 tsp vanilla flavoring**
❖ **4 Tbsp red wine**
❖ **3 Tbsp chopped
    pistachio nuts**

Cut 4 squares of heavy-duty aluminum foil and place 3 pear halves on each. Heat the lemon rind and juice, syrup, vanilla, and wine until boiling, then spoon the mixture all over the fruit. Wrap the foil around the pears to seal them completely.

Cook the pears over a preheated medium-hot grill for 5 to 8 minutes, until they are hot and tender but firm. Open each packet and brush the juices over the fruit. Sprinkle a few chopped pistachio nuts over each portion, and serve.

Chocolate-filled Pears

*The chocolate melts in the pear to make a pool of sauce. If you prefer,
use drained canned pear halves in place of fresh ones.*

Serves 8
Preparation time: 15 minutes
Cooking time: 10 minutes

❖ **4 large, very ripe pears,
peeled, halved, and
cored**

❖ **¾ cup grated semi-sweet
chocolate**
❖ **4 Tbsp chopped
hazelnuts, toasted**

Cut 8 large squares of heavy-duty aluminum foil and put a pear half, cored side up, on each. Fill the cores with chocolate and top with hazelnuts. Gather the foil, pouch style, around the pears and seal well at the top.

Preheat the grill to medium-hot. Stand the pouches on the rack for about 10 minutes, moving them around (but not turning them over) occasionally, or until the chocolate has melted and the pears are warmed through. Serve immediately.

Tropical Fruit Kebobs with Cardamom Butter

*Many kinds of fruit can be cooked on skewers. Cooking is not
really a problem as all you are doing is heating the fruit through, caramelizing the natural fruit sugars,
and giving it a new kind of smoky flavor. Serve with vanilla ice-cream.*

Serves 4
Preparation time: 15 minutes
Cooking time: 8 to 10 minutes

◇ **2 large ripe mangoes**
◇ **Four 1-inch slices fresh
  pineapple**
◇ **2 bananas**
◇ **2 kiwi fruits**
◇ **8 Tbsp (1 stick) unsalted
  butter**

◇ **¼ cup granulated brown
  sugar**
◇ **8 cardamom pods, seeds
  only**
◇ **½ tsp ground cinnamon**
◇ **Pinch of freshly grated
  nutmeg**
◇ **½ tsp grated lemon rind**
◇ **Crushed cardamom
  seeds, to serve**
◇ **Lemon rind, to garnish**
◇ **Vanilla ice cream, to serve**

Cut the mangoes in half and remove the pits. Remove the flesh from the skin in chunks about 1 inch in size. (Any smaller remaining pieces of mango can be covered, refrigerated,and eaten for breakfast the next day.) Peel, and remove the core from the pineapple and cut into chunks. Cut the bananas into 1-inch slices; peel and

quarter the kiwi fruits. Thread the fruit onto metal skewers, or wooden skewers that have been soaked in water for 30 minutes.

Melt the butter in a small pan and add the sugar, stirring constantly until the sugar has melted. Crush the cardamom seeds with a mortar and pestle and add to the hot butter along with the cinnamon, nutmeg, and lemon rind. Keep warm.

Preheat the barbecue coals to medium-hot, baste the fruit with the butter mixture, and place the skewers on an oiled rack. Cook, turning once, and basting frequently, until the fruit has begun to brown on the outside but is not too soft on the inside, about 8 to 10 minutes. Drizzle over any remaining butter, serve with crushed cardamom seeds, and garnish with lemon rind.

Orchard Fruit Kebobs with Gingered Rice Wine Sauce

*For a Far-Eastern feeL, you could try serving this sauce
with Tropical Fruit Kebobs (see page 00). You can also substitute your
favorite fruits, or fruits in season for those suggested here.*

Serves 4
Preparation time: 15 minutes
Cooking time: 8 to 10 minutes

❖ **2 tart apples such as
   Granny Smith**
❖ **1 to 2 Tbsp lemon juice**
❖ **2 nectarines, ripe but
   still firm**

❖ **4 plums, about 1½-
   inches long**
❖ **½ cup rice wine**
❖ **2 Tbsp grated fresh
   ginger**
❖ **1 Tbsp finely chopped
   candied ginger**
❖ **½ cinnamon stick**
❖ **Pinch sugar**

Cut the apples into 6 wedges, remove the cores and coat the cut edges in a little lemon juice. Peel the nectarines by dipping in boiling water for 20 seconds, then cool under running water; the skins should slip off easily, and cut each nectarine into 6 wedges. Remove the pits. Toss with lemon juice. Pit the plums and cut each in half. Arrange all the fruit together in a dish.

Put the remaining ingredients for the marinade in a small saucepan and bring just to boiling point. Pour over the fruit and leave to cool.

Using a slotted spoon, scoop the fruit out of the marinade and thread onto metal skewers, or wooden skewers that have been soaked in water for 30 minutes. Strain the remaining marinade into a small saucepan and boil until syrupy.

Preheat the barbecue coals to medium-hot and place the skewers on an oiled rack. Cook, turning once, until the fruit has begun to brown on the outside but is not too soft on the inside, about 8 to 10 minutes. Pour over the gingered rice wine syrup to serve.

Apples with Fruit and Nuts

*Thick, spicy slices of grilled apple are served with orange-flavored cream
cheese spiked with pecans and dates.*

Serves 6
Preparation time: 15 minutes
Cooking time: 10 minutes

❖ **4 Tbsp (½ stick) unsalted
   butter**
❖ **1 tsp ground cinnamon**
❖ **1 tsp ground cardamom**
❖ **6 crisp dessert apples,
   cored**
❖ **2 Tbsp granulated brown
   sugar**

❖ **1 cup cream cheese**
❖ **Finely grated rind and
   juice of 1 small orange**
❖ **Confectioners' sugar, to
   taste**
❖ **¼ cup finely chopped
   pecans**
❖ **¼ cup finely chopped
   dates**
❖ **Cream cheese, to serve**

Melt the butter and stir in the spices. Cut the apples into thick rings. Brush the mixture over both sides of the apple slices. Sprinkle with the brown sugar.

Blend the cream cheese with the orange rind and juice and confectioners' sugar. Fold in the pecans and dates. Cover until needed.

Arrange the apple slices on the preheated medium-hot grill and cook for about 10 minutes, turning occasionally, or until golden brown and still crisp. Serve topped with a spoonful of cream cheese.

Index